# From Here . . .
# To There . . .

*An Illustrated Memoir*
*of a Swiss Childhood*

ELLEN CARNEY

# From Here...To There...
## An Illustrated Memoir of a Swiss Childhood

Library of Congress Number: 2006927655
International Standard Book Number: 1-932864-86-5

*Printed at*
Masthof Press
*219 Mill Road*
*Morgantown, PA 19543-9516*

# TABLE OF CONTENTS

# Famous Last Words

This project started out as a dare. Remember the Milchchübeli served with each cup of coffee in Switzerland? And how the covers are decorated and therefore collected like baseball cards? Well, stupidly I ventured that I could draw as naively as Appenzeller folk artists who had their works featured on such crème covers.

"Do it!" was David's challenge.

To everyone's and my own amazement my response wasn't too bad. But it wasn't my own thing—these pictures of rural Appenzeller life. So I decided to concentrate on some of my childhood memories, on events which have changed or no longer exist, and made impressions on me.

What I depict spans the 1930s and 1940s, and what I remember of these years was put on paper in 1993-1995. When I wrote the text in 2002-2003 I became aware of some contradiction between my pictorial and written accounts. So, for ex., in Sunntigsjass the women seem to drink from cups while in the text I have them drink from glasses. Not essential in itself—but you might find some more of these inconsistencies. Trust the text—more reflection has gone into it.

Pronunciation rules are hard to come by. Perhaps you should ask a Swiss to help you say the few "Mundart" (vernacular, hard to translate, "way of the mouth") words of my period which I have added for authenticity. It is possible that even some of these expressions have become archaic since the language has changed even more than customs.

ä or ae approximately pronounced like a (as the article)
ei     ″   ″   ″         I         I
ö or oe   ″   ″   ″       as in grown
ü or ue    ″   ″   ″    Nuremberg (no English equivalent)
                           or French "tu"

In good old middle age fashion I did not sign the drawings with my name—but there is a telltale identification in most. Not a carnation or a rose, but a patriotic symbol and one alluding to my family's occupation. You be the puzzle solver or detective. This is one of my follies that you can interact with.

Thus spake
Ellen

# Sunntigsjass
# Sunday's Card Game

**J**f the Swiss Germans share one passion, it is the national pastime of Jasse. A card game played with suits of roses, bells, acorns, and shields, devoid of any female insignia. Instead, the cards illustrate a social stratification of Under (underling), Ober (upperclass) and Köenig (king). Both men and women catch this Jasse fever. Tournaments are held on local and regional levels and cultivate in the annual crowning of a Jasse Köenig. The rules of the game are a cross of whist and pinochle.

Jasse, for men, was the pretext for a night out and in rural areas especially, a reunion on Sunday afternoon in a local Wirtschaft (taproom).

I was initiated into this tradition during my vacation with grandparents, countryfolk; in contrast to my parents, first generation city slickers who, in part, had already discovered new recreational possibilities beside playing cards on a Sunday afternoon.

My paternal grandfather disappeared regularly, guests or no guests in the house, to walk cane in hand at least half an hour to meet his buddies in one of their favorite watering holes. They were called Krone (crown), Leue (lion), or Blume (flower) among many exotic names, and one of them could be found in every village. They advertised themselves with beautifully gilded insignia (bearing the sculpted image of their name) that hung out over the street. At supper grandpa would regale us with tales of the marvelous (or lousy) "hands" he bad been dealt and of his triumphs despite his partner's ineptitude at understanding his strategy signals. Losses occurred only due to bad luck, it seemed.

My maternal grandmother went with her partner on his outings, hoping that eventually she would be needed as a fourth player. Personally I loathed accompanying her to one of these beer reeking places filled with clouds of smoke from Stumpe (cigars) and Brissago (a super long cigarillo with a straw in the middle, typical of Switzerland). No matter which neighboring village we visited on foot, the Leue, Krone or Schlössli (little castle) were hardly distinguishable except for their insignia: darkish wood paneling, small windows with checkered curtains, sturdy chairs and tables; heavy ashtrays and cardboard coasters, both advertising beer, and of course a Jassteppich, a green felt "carpet" for the game on each table. A plate of rolls or Nussgipfel (crescent shaped nut paste filled Danish) and perhaps a bowl of hard boiled eggs on the tables for non-players. Not much art work, but a taxidermied antlered stag head, or a plaque of membership or recognition from some organization. Customarily there was the Stammtisch—a table reserved for regulars who dropped in daily for their beer and politicking, or for reading the newspaper clamped in its wooden spreader.

The human scene did not much differ either from place to place. The card players scowled at or scolded each other for missed opportunities, the opponents gloated in their success. And both kept score on small slateboards: one hundred a mark on the topline of a large Z, fifty on the diagonal and twenties on the bottom line, the rest spelled out in numerals and eventually added up. While shuffling they often told jokes which I did not understand until much later when I caught on to their risqué nature. I especially disliked the men's becoming too familiar with the waitress, always dressed in black with a white half apron covering her deep pocketed money belt. I watched it grow fatter as the afternoons wore on and she added people's tab from memory without any mechanical help. Perhaps there were some grandmotherly women present, drinking café crème from high stemmed glasses which somehow conveyed an air of sophistication. As a rule they knew each other, and shared a table, gossiped and in good industrious Swiss fashion: knitted. Even the waitress might have knitted during quiet interludes. Hardly a sign of kids. Either they played on swings outside or stayed home alone. Supervision was not a big deal, kids took care of themselves. So I felt like a fish out of water with my glass of raspberry syrup and Nussgipfel, having my cheeks tweeked and being asked how I liked my country vacation.

The parties would break up toward dusk; after all we all had to still walk home on unlit streets and lanes, often through dense woods. The fresh air never smelled so good.

# Milchma
# Milkman

Except for the villa district on the Zürichberg very few houses in the city had garden plots. Most of these were one family dwellings built many years ago, all in a row by factory owners for their laborers or more recently by coops. Their front gardens were handkerchief-sized and mainly utilitarian, producing vegetables from early peas, to lettuce to late oyster plants. Apple, peach and cherry poachers were deterred by wooden fences. They also kept a few rosebushes safe, perhaps some gladioli and sunflowers as well. The real showy flowers were grown on windowsills, geraniums and all kinds of begonias.

People in the apartment houses only had abutting backyards, impersonal spaces where an occasional weed poked through the gravel and moss grew between cobblestones. A courtyard with installations to beat carpets, dry laundry, and air mattresses and pillows during spring cleaning. A place for the kids to hang out after school, hop-scotch or plan some mischief.

But these courtyards were also the place where many women of the neighborhood bought their milk from the milkman. At fairly regular times each morning he would appear with his hand-pushed, paw-drawn (by one of those strong Swiss dogs), or bicycle-attached cart weighted down with steel milk drums. And rang his customers' doorbells. They then emerged from all over to have their daily supply of milk measured out with liter ladles into special Milchchesseli (small aluminum kettle with lid) or fat milk pitchers. If a regular customer failed to show up, the milkman found her container and instructions in a special cubbyhole behind her built-in mailbox in the lobby.

Earlier in the morning the milkman had collected those milk drums either himself or had them delivered to his store (where his wife was now selling cheese, butter and eggs) by truck from a central Molkerei (dairy). Which in turn had gone out the night before to pick up full (and deliver empty ones) standing outside barns or on collection platforms along country roads. To live near a Molkerei was to wake up very early in the morning: the clanking of those milk drums equaled the noise of New York garbage trucks.

Since all of this occurred before the time of pasteurization, and before glass bottles and those hard to open cartons came along, the milk had to be processed fairly quickly before it turned sour. So, as a rule moms boiled it almost immediately to kill the bacteria. After the milk cooled, a thick wrinkly skin formed on top which some of us loved and others hated to see slip into our coffee. For those the milk

was poured through a strainer…which was ooky to clean afterwards.

During the war we often kept the Milchchesseli in cold running water for some hours, no refrigeration then! Because the milk was not homogenized, its yellow cream would rise to the top for us to be able to skim it. After we had collected a few days' worth and kept it fresh in cold water, we either whipped it for some dessert, or churned it into butter to give us respite from the orange hued margarine. Oleo was tinted so that it could not be palmed off as butter. Each package contained an orange dye capsule which burst when you kneaded the margarine into a presentable shape to serve.

In retrospect it actually seems amazing that during the war milk and milk products were strictly rationed in the country of the postcard cows. By American standards we consumed very little milk.

We children drank café au lait with meals right from the get-go; no cereal for breakfast, but a slice of bread, oleo and jam. Even after WWII when my children asked for milk to go with their meal in a restaurant, alarm bells would go off; nobody had ever made such a strange request. When they were eventually served a glass of hot milk they of course would not drink this unusual tasting stuff. (By the way, a request for a glass of plain water was received with similar astonishment by the waitress.)

Chocolate, too, was rationed; this we could understand because Switzerland neither produced cacao nor large quantities of sugar from beets. Cane sugar had to be imported but imports were nonexistent for years. So, chocolate bars became coveted presents from grandparents who no longer indulged. I never asked why cheese also should be rationed—did they slaughter the cows to provide us with meat and thereby make everything else a scarce commodity?

These days the milkman no longer rings doorbells. Not only because most courtyards have been converted into parking spaces, but because milk now comes superpasteurized in cardboard boxes from the supermarket as do all other groceries, from vegetables and fruit to meat and wine . . . and paper towels, cheese and frozen pizza. Mr. Anliker most likely had to go out of business. Probably too has disappeared the Schabzigerma, the peddler from Glarus who sold the green herb cheese door to door from his wooden rack. Perhaps a few people mourn the loss of these institutions but many more take for granted the plethora of chocolate candies for snacking after school. We were happy with a Stängeli (fingerlong round pieces of chocolate with hazelnut cream, wrapped in a silver paper) and a piece of bread and butter... a feast if sprinkled with sugar. Swiss children are now as familiar with Mars Bars, Baby Ruth and Tootsie Rolls as Americans with the Matterhorn imitating Toblerone or a bar of Lindt chocolate. The Swiss may eat cornflakes and the Americans Muesli... globalization of goods and customs!

# Spring in Zürich

S pring (not necessarily the astronomically fixed season, but the one which feels like a new beginning) brought us and still does, two occasions to celebrate: Oschtere (Easter) and Sächsilüte (six o'clock churchbell ringing).

Even though most children in my days helped dye the Easter eggs, it was still the bunny who mysteriously hid them all over the apartment. I did the most exciting dyeing with my grandmother who lived in a small country village. Together we searched for pretty weeds and wild primroses (Schlüsselblümli) which poked their heads out of the soil just about that time. These we arranged and patiently tied around the eggs with raffia or string. We boiled the bundles in a brew of onion skins which grandma had saved over many months. Beautiful, dark brown eggs with white leaf or lovely flower silhouettes emerged from this mess.

On Easter morning, kids of all ages traditionally congregate under arcades along the river in the old city to engage in Eiertütschis (egg tapping). They bring what they consider their eggs with the hardest shells for tapping, or more accurately knocking top and bottom of their egg against top and bottom of someone else's egg. Whoever's egg remains intact or is the least cracked, acquires the more damaged one.

Teenagers are not usually keen on taking home many cracked eggs for salad and leave this particular activity to younger kids. Instead they offer their eggs partially exposed in heavily gloved hands to grown ups willing to forcefully toss and hopefully land a coin in it. If the coin glances off the shell, it becomes the egg owner's booty. If it finds its mark by penetrating the shell, the coin tosser takes egg and coin . . . theoretically. Adults, mostly fathers showing off for their children, don't hold the loser to the bargain.

By the way, Easter Monday is a holiday as well.

The second spring celebration occurs after Easter, closer to the Spring Equinox and also lasts two days: the traditional Sächsilüte.

In the middle ages artisans worked during the winter months until daylight became too dim. In order for them not to have to work too long as the days lengthened, churchbells were rung at six o'clock in the evening. It was a reminder to stop working but also a sign for the spouses to prepare supper. They had been exhorted similarly at eleven in the morning, to cook the midday meal.

This labor-linked tradition is acted out on the second day of the festivities. The Guilds, oldtime unions, parade on both sides of the Limmat, in occupation specific garb and bearing the tools of their trade. Thus, the bakers wear the black and white checkered pants, white coats and pillbox caps as they distribute rolls from floats all along the parade route. The tailors in gray tophats capnap spectators' hats with huge

scissors, making children scream and adults laugh: they know the hat will be returned. The merchant guild used to parade with their insignia, camels borrowed from the zoo, symbols of their trading far and wide. Butchers passed out sausages while threatening with big cleavers.

Districts which have been more recently incorporated into the city limits take part showing off a characteristic industry (like wine making or milling wood) or a landmark (such as a watertower) on elaborate floats.

It is a colorful spring flower spectacle. Some marchers carry armfuls of daffodils and tulips which are bestowed on them by friends and mostly female relatives. The Monday parade, as well as the guilds themselves, are a strictly male preserve. A hangover from the times when women were to be found only in their own kitchen or someone else's as a domestic. For years now a group of professional women, having formed their own guild, have sought the right to join this parade . . . in vain. Recently they have organized their own along the same route, on the same day.

Females may participate in the Sunday, coed children's parade wearing either fancy period costumes (Biedermeier) or traditional Swiss regional dresses (Tracht). Proudly even under raingear or heavy wraps, depending on the whim of Saint Peter, boys dress similarly.

However, they seem to prefer appearing as ululating Indians swinging tomahawks, or as some other exotic personage. My seven-year-old brother suffered one of his first big disappointments when my parents discovered that he had bought a real live axe for the event with money he had begged from friends and strangers. Naturally mother returned it to the hardware store. Probably giving the owner quite a piece of her mind. Poor Fritz had to do with a cardboard replica. Marching bands and horse-drawn wagons festooned with flowers are interspersed among the children to help them keep pace or give them a lift when their legs get tired. Unfortunately, children have also been trampled by horses. At the end of the circuit, everyone is regaled with a Bratwurst and a crusty roll.

The adult Monday parade ends more dramatically. While some of the guilds repair to their landmark headquarters (Zunfthaus) in the old city, the merchant Camel clan gathers on the Sächsilüte meadow near the lake, formerly with camels now on horses. There, with sabers drawn and white robes flowing, they gallop around a huge cottony snowman with a basket hat and packed with explosives towering on a high stack of blazing wood. Everybody anxiously awaits the moment when the effigy of winter (dä Bögg) is torn apart. Because the time it takes for the head or chest to catapult off into the air supposedly predicts summer's weather. If the bang occurs quickly, beautiful weather is in store—a long wait means rain and a summer which does not come up to seasonal expectations. Of course, the snowman's predictions may not be totally reliable if the pyre has been rained on and the flames roar up reluctantly despite dousings of kerosene.

Even if it rains on the ceremony and the galloping horses kick up mud, many people prefer watching this performance live rather than on TV, at least once in their life.

# School in the 30's

**W**ell, it was different.

First off, I had to learn a new language. Switching from the Zürich dialect to high German (Hochdeutsch) was not easy. Some words had no resemblance in the two languages. But Hochdeutsch had to be mastered in order for us to learn how to read—anything from instructions, to books, application forms, from ballots to ads. The Swiss German dialects are many and defy organized phonetics.

Secondly, for nine years most of us walked to school, no matter how far, city or countryside, dark or light, rain or sunshine. The bells rang at 8 o'clock. At 12 noon we hiked back home for the main meal of the day with the whole family, including dad . . . to return by 2:00 PM for the afternoon session lasting until 4:00. Except on Wednesdays and Saturdays when we enjoyed a free afternoon.

And third: You would not find a Swiss flag in any classroom. We never pledged allegiance, or recited a school prayer at the beginning of the day. Nobody ever went to assembly either, or knew a principal. Instead of being decorated with the portrait of a national hero, our walls were hung with a print by Anker who painted idealized family scenes and the famous St. Gotthard postal coach careening down the steep mountain road.

School was serious business, and began for most of us at age 7. Some lucky ones by then had spent a year or so in Gvätterlischuel (tinkering school, better known as Kindergarten) with emphasis on tinkering rather than the beginnings of formalized learning the basics, like the ABC. That was reserved for first grade, when we learned sounding out words phonetically; or building words with the aid of a "setzchaschte," a box of moveable letters like the early printers used.

Our first real reading efforts were concentrated on colorfully illustrated story sheets which we kept carefully in a folder to prevent dog ears. These folders left the classroom only once: to show off our achievement to parents on the day the story cycle had ended and everything had to be handed back to serve another bunch of first graders.

First graders differentiated themselves from Kindergarteners by wearing a Thek whereas those had only worn a small snack bag over their shoulders the way some women now carry their pocketbooks. This Thek was a boxy but slim leather backpack. It, and the pencilbox

with the sliding top which we toted in it for the six years of elementary school, were the only items our parents had to supply; everything else, books, paper, pens was free. The pencilbox was actually a "Fädereschachtle" (penbox) because we were never allowed to use pencils. Together, the Thek and the box revealed either our taste or our parents' affluence. Never more so than on a boy's Thek. Its backflap was generally covered with some animal fleece—fake leopard being the most prestigious.

The pencilbox became useful in second grade when we learned how to print. Not with pencil and eraser but with pen and ink. The pen consisted of a wooden holder into which we inserted steel nibs, new ones from time to time. While transporting the ink-filled nib from the inkwell, sunk into the top of our slanted desklid, to our paper, we beginners lost many a Tölgge (blotch) which had to be soaked up from the wood. That's why the box also contained a Tintelumpe, (inkrag). Blotting paper helped with the smears on the paper. To erase them or mistakes, we carried erasers which unfortunately also rubbed holes in the paper. That is why we were encouraged to merely put parentheses around errors and continue with the work. Few of us did, being too embarrassed to admit to a mistake. We preferred recopying the page. Having to work with a cleanly wiped pen and ink at our earliest writing stages disciplined us to think twice before committing anything to paper, especially in math.

We did not print for long before cursive writing lessons, or calligraphy as we called it, were inflicted upon us. The dullest and most disliked of all our subjects. But we practiced it daily while the teacher droned a rhythm accompanied by the flick of a bamboo stick up-down-up-shade-down-up . . . . The report card would comment on the legibility of our efforts until 9th grade; sometimes anecdotally, sometimes numerically: 1 failure, 6 excellent. My 4th to 6th grade teacher was himself bored with this exercise and played Bach's Brandenburg Concertos over and over; or read poetry by Nietzsche. Did he think we would understand it?

Yes, our teachers accompanied each class of *25* pupils or more during three years, even in secondary school. (Woe to us if we did not like him or her, or vice versa!) They taught all subjects, academic as well as music, art and phys ed, except for home economics or shop, which were offered starting in 3rd grade. The girls learned how to crochet, knit and eventually sew. I'll always remember my first project, knitting a blue, sock-like bag for Znüni (9 o'clock snack) with five needles. This skill came in handy when we had to knit socks for the Swiss army during the war, in gymnasium, to the professors' lectures. Taking notes was a bit complicated.

No group projects were assigned. Not even in gymnasium, prep-type school prior to university, were students allowed hands-on science projects. The emphasis was on learning facts and dates. What caused wind or rain, how much cotton Egypt exported, the still incomplete atomic table, and when and where (but not why) those bellicose Swiss fought battles for their own confederation or foreign potentates.

Many kids may have liked gymnastics, but most liked recess, two of them in the morning, one in the afternoon. During the first one we usually ate our Znüni, Butterbrot or an apple, before we played at hopscotch, skipping rope, Fangis (catch me) or practiced our fancy ball skills against the school-house wall. Disputes were settled by a supervising teacher on a rotating basis. All classes were on the playground at the same time. Staying behind in the room during recess was either a privilege (if we liked the teacher) or a punishment, and in both cases involved erasing or washing black boards. In the front of the room there were two moveable slate boards either hung above each other against the walls, or on wheels. Both types could be swiveled and written on both sides.

Mentioning punishment: Until 6th grade it was quite common for teachers to whack our left hand (we were all made into right handers) with a square ruler for misbehaving. Some clever victims rubbed their palms with onions to produce a good-sized swelling which could make a teacher pretty uncomfortable. If a supervisor from the Board of Education got wind of such an incident, we could expect monitors for some time, checking on the teacher's temper.

Aside from minor pranks, such as talking, pulling pigtails or apron strings, passing notes or throwing a paper airplane when the teacher's back was turned, behavior hardly ever got out of control. And never merited more than writing a sentence 100 times, staying after school, or standing outside the classroom door during a fun subject. If you're like my brother, though, you would simply go home instead of cooling your heels outside the door—thus becoming a hero to your more daring classmates. Usually, however, punishment evoked so much teasing from peers that most of us were shamed into "being good."

If we liked a teacher, we showed off during visits from supervisors who appeared regularly during the year. A dentist only came once to inspect our teeth and refer those in need to a health clinic. But the Luustante (lice aunt) searched our heads more frequently . . . yes, for lice. And monthly we swallowed our brown iodine pill because goiters were endemic in Switzerland before iodized salt hit the shelves.

Then there was "Elteretag" (parent day) which we anticipated with trepidation since it was a kind of oral testing day. Were we going to embarrass ourselves with wrong answers in front of all these people ? Were our mothers going to be dressed appropriately, without an apron, so we would not be teased later? Two things we could be sure of on that day. One: the custodian had swept the dark brown floor with kerosene-soaked sawdust. And Two: a basket of Examewegge (examination rolls), distinctively shaped for this occasion exclusively, was the reward for our ordeal.

Each season of the year had its one-or-two-week long vacation. Summer's was five weeks and the school year started in spring. Just prior to summer vacation we were usually treated to an excursion, ever farther afield as we grew older. Parents seldom chaperoned—there were no aides; so a friend or the wife of the rare male teacher would accompany the expedition in elementary school. The girls jealously competed for holding hands with this visitor but never with the authority figure. Curiously, we never visited a museum or any other site directly relating to our studies. No field trips in those days. The yearly trek, however, involved a train or boat ride and lots of hiking and singing. As a rule, we brought our own food in a small Rucksack (backpack).

After six years of primary school we graduated without fanfare or special celebration into three years of secondary school, often in the same building. Those aspiring eventually to an academic career went off to gymnasium for six years, separate complexes for boys and girls near the University and the Technical Institute where Albert Einstein studied. Additionally there was a trade-oriented curriculum for slow learners and those not wanting to pursue any academics.

There were some visible distinctions between an elementary and a secondary pupil. The Thek was abandoned for a "Mappe," a very clumsy briefcase type affair. Imagine two briefcases connected to each other so that when closed the compartments faced each other   and then imagine opening this contraption (without spilling anything) by flipping one half over the other.

By now, both compartments held textbooks as well as notebooks for each subject. Also the leather etui with pen, pencil and eraser that replaced the pencilbox.

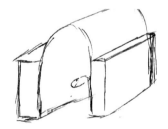

The girls shed their aprons. We felt grown up but were at a loss for what to do with the ubiquitous handkerchief. French was introduced in 7th grade. In gymnasium, which was not co-ed like the regular public, school, we started out with Latin instead, which stayed with us through the Iliad until graduation, 6½ years later. In this curriculum two or more modern languages or classical Greek were introduced additionally in 8th and 9th grade. It was a heavy load. Only one half of my initial class of 20 graduated; and only a few of those continued studying at the university. Which means that about 10 women (there were 2 classes) from the canton of Zurich received higher degrees from that year.

After secondary school you still had the opportunity to enter the Seminar (teacher training school) or study to be a social worker in the Frauenfachschule (women's career training school). Most 9th graders, however, left school. Their education was far from over, though. They had to decide on what career to pursue, find someone who would allow them to absolve a one-or-two-year-apprenticeship in their establishment. This on the job training, be it in sale or tailoring, cooking or book-keeping, was augmented by pertinent course work in night school. Wages amounted to pocket money and necessitated that these future professionals live with their parents for another few years. Unless they decided to become proficient in French or Italian and found a "volontair" (au pair type) job in another part of Switzerland, where they worked for room and board and a small stipend.

At the end of each school year we scrubbed and sandpapered our sins out of our desks, double seat arrangements which were bolted together, 4 sets one behind the other, three or four rows to a room. Ink stains, initials or "cribs" had to be eradicated. And the teachers inspected the books we might have to hand back for recycling in another class, for any blemish we had inflicted on them. We were fined according to the gravity of our carelessness.

Education was indeed serious business.

# Trains

My family seemed to have an aversion to travelling by public transportation. Therefore, aside from a few trips to grandparents during the war, my main memories of the SBB (Schweiz Bundes Bahn) are from observing the closed railroad crossings while waiting in the family car. I watched, sometimes a bit intimidated by the noise and rush of air, how the electric locomotives rumbled a snake of passenger and freight cars past the lowered red and white striped pole barriers, which were reinforced with a curtain of metal chains hanging to the ground to prevent small whatevers from getting on the tracks. These barriers were handcranked, up and down from early morning until night. So it stands to reason that the operator, often a woman, sometimes a husband and wife team, practically lived on the spot. But not slept! As a matter of fact, the last of these crossings were abolished in favor of mechanized ones, when a sleeping guard caused a collision between bus and train which resulted in the death of many passengers.

But while the old system was in place, the crossing guards nested in a one-room cabin with many comforts of home. I was fascinated to no end by the handkerchief-size gardens which surrounded these little houses. Replete with vegetables and flowers, a bench, and a stack of wood for the stove—all fenced in. A veritable doll-house scene where kids could play safely while mother sat, knitting between tending to the needs of the train schedule.

Trains were announced by an earsplitting alarm, a chattering metal contraption on the wall or a mushroom-like free-standing bell. The signal was relayed from the nearest station in time for the barrier to be lowered, according to timetable . . . and Swiss trains are renowned for being punctual. The noise of the alarm was deafening enough for all to heed, to stop the car, get off the bicycle, or refrain from crossing the tracks on foot. I always wondered if the cows understood the meaning of the signal as well—there were no cowcatchers on the locomotives, yet I never heard of cow casualties. Perhaps it was the famous Swiss breed dogs' job to keep their herd safe and off the tracks.

Even more incredulous than the guard houses were the shelters and gardens outside larger train stations or where tracks needed to be switched to dispatch trains into the direction of their destination. They were peaceful islands of sanity among mechanical monsters and noise, where, incredibly, flowers bloomed and cabbages got fat, or smoke curled out of a diminutive chimney in the winter. And if you happened to wave from the lowered window, somebody probably waved back.

# Rekrutenschule
# Basic Training

In my days, 60 years ago, when men reached the age of 18, they were ready for obligatory military service. If found sound in mind and spirit, they underwent several months of basic training; then attended periodic refresher courses until the age of 40, but remained soldiers until the age of 60, ready to be called to active duty on a moment's notice. Additionally they proved their marksmanship once a year in a municipal shooting range and had to go for further training if they failed the test.

In Zürich, the young recruits assembled in the Kaserne. They had their heads shaved and were issued a very heavy, stiff, green woolen uniform—one size fits all—a steel helmet and a rifle with bayonet, and a tornister, a fleece-covered, boxy leather backpack which just empty weighed a ton. It would be loaded down further according to strict specifications with personal items, clothes, and draped over with a voluminous but tightly rolled coat (Kaput). A mess kit dangled from a hook. All of this paraphernalia was kept at home in mothballs. The rifle too, with some ammo, stayed with the soldier so that a fully functional army could be constituted within hours of call-up.

The Kasernen yard echoed with the sound of heavily nailed shoes drilling. The future soldiers shuffled their guns from arm to arm, saluted officers, marched in place, or to and fro, turning corners in precision and doing calisthenics to shrill commands. I never understood how all this to-do would help defend a country. For the target practice or maneuvers, the recruits marched in step (but not in goosestep), singing, to a vast commons outside the city, the Allmend, where flocks of sheep grazed in quiet times. At night, if the men were not too tired, they would hang out the barrack windows singing or whistling at passing women until lights-out.

Some men were selected for special training according to their background. Farmers' sons might be assigned to horse details, mountaineers to ski patrols in the alps. There were troops on bicycles, pontoon-builders, while some worked with homing pigeons which are now replaced by electronic gysmos. There were medics and those with advanced education might graduate to officers' school (and then join the ranks of bank officials). What fascinated us, and had us watch through the iron fence around the barracks, were the bald recruits drilling and the music corps practicing.

Men ineligible for active service and Swiss men abroad unable to participate in repeater courses paid a heavy military tax. However, many an unsuspecting citizen stepping off an airplane or train from a foreign country, found himself in the ranks of the army the following day absolving his civic duty. His passport at customs or the frontier had identified him to authorities

For some local men these periodic refresher courses represented a form of vacation, a chance to get to the country, to the mountains, and to nightly live it up with a bunch of high-spirited companions. Furthermore, their homecoming was often an extended family celebration at which they were feted like heroes.

No locks are shorn these days; earrings are tolerated; the uniform looks comfortable and fits; the Tornisters have found their way to antique stores and as a matter of fact, from time to time a referendum is launched for a vote to abolish compulsory service and to leave home security in the hands of volunteers. Justification for this thinking: The army is ineffective in modern warfare when a small country like Switzerland can be overrun in minutes. (Other factions want to extend the training period since the means of war and defense have become more complicated.)

Historically, we expected Hitler to swallow us in WWII but he spared us for a host of reasons other than the fact that the Alps had been prepared as a reduit for military hold out. Before him, Napoleon had believed Switzerland to be easy prey. But he later dubbed it the puss blister of Europe and withdrew his troops. These days, members of the Swiss military act as peacekeepers under UN auspices. Swiss men still constitute the Papal Guard, a remnant of the Swiss past when men without a future hired on as fighters for foreign potentates. Lord Nelson is reputed to have been shot by a Swiss marksman in the battle of Trafalgar, and who defended the Bastille? Swiss, of course.

# Märt
# Market

The selection of fresh fruit and vegetables was quite limited. Not only because stores lacked the space and the means of keeping them fresh but also because in those days, they only dealt with local (not imported) and seasonal produce. Whatever they did carry, they sold on the sidewalk outside their premises on artfully arranged tables. An awning protected the saleslady with the cash apron, the scales and the wares from rain and shine.

There is always the exception to the rule: Somewhere in the neighborhood there may have been a "Südfrüchtelade" (a store with fruit from the south). Long salamis, hunks of prosciutto dangled from the ceilings, black wheels of Parmigian were stacked on the counter with a few straw-covered bottles of Chianti. The owner invariably had an Italian name, and a largely Italian clientele finding there those long spaghetti in blue wrapper. But he, too, displayed his early imported tomatoes, pepperoni, zucchinis, figs and oranges and things we did not even know, then, on the trottoir (pavement). Not merely to tempt passers-by, but for lack of space. Everything was dismantled and carried inside every evening, to be reassembled again each morning, except in subzero weather. Not on Sundays, though, no store opened Sunday or on holidays, except emergency pharmacies on a rotating basis.

A third alternative to obtain fresh produce was Market day. Traditionally truckfarmers and gardeners brought their products every Tuesday and Friday into the city and set up their stands along a designated market street and square. Already at eight o'clock throngs of shoppers arrived and inspected the heads of lettuce, potatoes, string beans, carrots and berries, whatever was in season, for freshness, size and price, all along the street. But somehow each housefrau was likely to return to her favorite vendor with whom she was on a last name basis and chatted about more than just the weather. Knowing the grower personally was an advantage not just during the war when they could insure your ration of eggs; they also added another handful of whatever to your purchase. Husband and wife managed the larger stands; but the men often disappeared to have a beer. Many smaller enterprises were headed by women only who had grown their produce in kitchen gardens. The pushcarts on which they had walked their assortment served as their stand. Whenever someone failed to occupy their allotted space, regular customers congregated and speculated on the reason for their provider's absence.

On Friday fresh fish was available as well, slightly separated from the main hubub; under trees and close to a fountain providing water to sprinkle the fish with . . . and to wash hands . . . oh, what a fishy smell . . . to this day it turns my stomach.

No matter what her social status or her budget, a woman rarely returned from the market without a bouquet of flowers, except in winter of course. Flowers and plants are part of the Swiss lifestyle, in private as well as in the public sphere. Every city employs an army of gardeners embellishing parks and squares with seasonally changing flower exhibits. City Fathers have distributed seeds and sponsored window box competitions among apartment dwellers. One year sunflowers reached for light from the windowsills in the narrow streets of the old city.

Market day still happens regularly from eight to eleven, rain or shine (or snow). Rain brings out waterproof gear, black oil cloth coats with hoods, then; the familiar yellow plastic coat, now. Colorful umbrellas protect the merchandise now as well as then, plus the newspaper aka wrapping paper, which had to be kept dry.

Winter market still means heavy coats and high boots and predominantly root crops: Beets, carrots, salsify and potatoes. As well as the ubiquitous cabbage, red and green and curly (savoy); some onions, perhaps woven in braids, and leeks; and of course apples with thick skins, like the Boskop with the yellow flesh so tasty for applesauce and Wähe, a Friday rectangular pie-like main meal for a meatless day. But no strawberries in November or fresh tomatoes in January. Perhaps an orange from Spain or Jaffa, a tangerine around Christmas. During winter it was back to canned peas and carrots or string beans, cherries, pears and apricots (both of which were dried too, as well as string beans), an occasional exotic fruit cocktail—all stuff you buy in the grocery store.

While I described some aspects of market days in the past tense, the institution operates to this day but on a reduced scale what with large supermarkets offering fresh, imported and frozen choices. Many women are no longer stay-at-homes and so have less leisure time to market during working hours, except on Saturdays. So, many providers had to adapt their growing and marketing strategies from retailing to wholesaling in order to survive . . . and stopped bothering with the market. Antique dealers have started to fill their niche.

# Buying Shoes before World War II

Like most purchases, other than food, buying shoes represented a major event in a family's life. One: Father had to be convinced that new shoes were necessary since he held the purse string to all expenditures; Two: Mother accompanied us to a store, a rare happening—going out together in the middle of the week; Three: We could show off in school. Not the new pair, but our Sunday ones into which we had predictably graduated once the school pair had begun to really pinch our toes. This meant that the Sunday shoes now became the every day pair, and a new, slightly too large pair had to take their place. Actually they were not just for Sunday, but also for dress up occasions, like going to the doctor or dentist, or on a rare visit to a relative.

There were no classes Wednesday afternoon. Shoe stores took advantage and stimulated business by handing out free balloons with each purchase. So midweek became the logical time for this transaction.

Not many styles were available. Laces or straps with a button, no loafers; colors: Brown or black, white for first communion. Before entering the store we picked our favorite pair in the show window, with mother's counsel of course. She did all the talking, as was the custom anywhere, and communicated our choice to one of the clerks in lab coats. They then started to move ladders (like the ones in movie libraries) along floor-to-ceiling shelves full up with labeled white boxes, until they located the one containing our pick. But just in case we or mother would change our mind, they tucked a few more under their arms for us to try on.

Sitting astride a boxlike stool they slipped the shoes on our feet with a shoehorn. We usually wore extra heavy socks or stockings for the occasion. To test the fit we were asked to walk around the store on carpeted floors. But the adults were not necessarily satisfied with our own assessment: They pinched our toes to determine how much room we had. Or as a last resort we were marched to the X-ray machine to reveal the ultimate truth. Especially if we had chosen patent leather which was generally deemed an unsuitable choice. But it was interesting to see our bones in this machine—the closest to a real live anatomy lesson we ever came. The practice has since been outlawed—because of dangerous rays the equipment emitted.

Just buying the shoes and flying the balloon was not the end of the Wednesday adventure. First, the shoes had to be buffed with waterproof polish. Then they had to be taken to the shoemaker who festooned the heels and toes with horseshoe curved steel pieces. They were to prevent the quick wearing down of the leather. Chances are, however, that the shoes had to be resoled anyway before we outgrew them totally, considering the amount of walking we did.

Occasionally we got rubber boots at the same time as the shoes, perhaps even red ones; or black galoshes to keep shoes and toes dry. A special treat was to get a pair of dark blue gym shoes to protect the turnhalle (gym) floor. They were never to be worn elsewhere, except when they were too small for our feet.

# Erster August
# First of August

**F**lags are the hallmark of August 1, a day steeped in tradition and legend. Flags are flown all year round, but they serve mainly decorative purposes on mountain tops, steam boats and on occasion, a church tower. The bright red square with the white cross livens the green (or white) countryside, gray city streets and certainly looks photogenic against the blue sky of calendar pages. Swiss love their flag, but don't pledge allegiance to it, not even on this day when it assumes a patriotic dimension and is flown everywhere, from ordinary buildings, across narrow streets in the old part of towns, and shines through votive candle glasses on windowsills.

On August 1, the Swiss commemorate the 1291 Rütlischwur (the oath on the meadow Rütli) when representatives of three cantons, Uri, Schwyz and Unterwalden laid the foundation of what would over hundreds of years evolve into Switzerland. Still today bonfires are customarily lit on mountaintops as a reminder that this is how the news of the event was announced over the region. During the day there are patriotic celebrations, at which speeches from all levels of government are heard, brass bands play, flags are tossed in the air, choral societies perform, perhaps an alphorn is blown, national costumes are resurrected out of mothballs . . . someone may even yodel. Beer flows freely, cervelats roast without let up. And fireworks proclaim the official end of the celebration but the beergardens remain open for a few more hours.

During some research I discovered that I was taught Swiss history, especially "the birth of the nation" according to the *White Book of Sarnen* compiled in 1470 with the sagas surrounding the beginnings of the confederation. As with the Gospels, written long after Jesus' death, many tales had by then been woven around the historical event. The legends were even more fancifully embroidered, exploited and popularized in a drama by the German Friedrich Schiller, and in an opera by the Italian composer Rossini. Its overture became the theme for the Lone Ranger.

According to the *White Book* the representatives of the three cantons met on a meadow on the shores of the Vierwaldstättersee in order to swear an oath to rid themselves of the Habsburg yoke and to give mutual assistance should there be hostile repercussions due to this decision.

This action was precipitated, so says a legend, by William Tell who one day refused to pay homage to the supremacy of the Habsburg bailiff Gessler in the guise of one of his hats hoisted on a pole in Altdorf's main square. His sentence was to shoot an apple off his son's head with one arrow from his bow. Being a crack sharpshooter he predictably split the apple in two, but was observed to slip a second arrow into his vest. Questioned by Gessler about the meaning of this action, he replied "Had I missed the apple on my son's head, I surely would not have missed you."

He spoke freely because he had been promised immunity if he spoke the truth. This threat proved too much for Gessler who had him taken prisoner and marched to his barge on the lake for his return to the castle in Küsnacht. There Tell would have been incarcerated for life. Happily, a heavy, but for this lake not unusual storm broke out, creating waves Gessler's soldiers could not master. In desperation they enlisted Tell's rowing skills. He knew the waters, agreed and steered the boat towards a flat plateau along the shore, jumped ship and hurried to a wide gully in a wooded area near the castle. There he ambushed and killed Gessler, thus starting events rolling.

Memorial chapels have been erected on both hallowed spots, the Tellsprung (where he jumped), and the Hohle Gasse (hollow lane). We school children were encouraged to save our pennies to buy the land of the Hohle Gasse so it could be converted into a national shrine.

Serious historians doubted these accounts early on but especially so after the appearances of Schiller and Rossini's concoctions. Because their own writing was incredibly dull, nobody heeded their alarm or was willing to debunk the colorful accounts. So, the true history of events, such as they are documented, were not discussed publicly until I too had been bathed in the romantic, patriotic version and our 6th class had made their pilgrimage to these shrines. There is a third monument, a huge statue in Altdorf, of Tell with his son by his side and a crossbow over his shoulder. We passed it yearly on my father's summer treks across an alpine pass or other. We did not stop to pay homage (Dad was in a hurry to test his driving skills and the car's performance on the serpentine curves) except the few times when my mother insisted on buying some Nussgipfel in the square's bakery (later, she discovered a crystal shop).

The true historical account is more likely contained in the "Bundesbrief" (Letter of Confederation) to which the representatives had sworn. It is written in Latin, (and therefore not likely composed by mere peasants) and merely states that henceforth the citizens of the area would no longer tolerate foreign judges. A concession which they had been granted already previously by Rudolf von Habsburg. It further

detailed the judicial process and the types of punishment that would be meted out uniformly with the alliance. The document even states that they would not cease to be vassals to whomever they were indentured. Essentially they only wanted to end the many fights among themselves and institute civil peace in the area.

The crossbow remains a mighty symbol for goods manufactured in Switzerland. Tell has become a personification of the Swiss spirit of defiance . . . and an engraving on the five Frank coin. Interestingly, both the U.S. and Switzerland share the melody of "God Save the Queen" for one of their patriotic songs "My Country 'tis of Thee" and "Heil Dir Helvetia."


I wish I had regularly bought and collected one of those Abzeichen (buttons) which are designed and sold specifically for this day each year, to benefit a charity. They would make quite an interesting display on a Swiss Antique Road Show.

# Grosi's Lädeli
# Grandma's Small Store

**M**y grandfather owned what would now be called a free-range chicken farm in the country. Such an enterprise was rather unusual in those days, because most chickens were raised sort of incidentally and as part of a typical farm, not an industry in itself. Therefore, chicken was not your every day protein; it was reserved for special occasions.

While Grandpa tended to the birds and their shelters, Grandma ran a small scale convenience store, a modest 7/11, in a room on the first floor of the three-story apartment house. In itself an oddity in an area of only one family farmhouses. It was the place where neighbors, mostly farmers and passing through handymen could, in a pinch, get what they had run out of before their next trip to a better-supplied store a few kilometers away.

Demands were simple; partly because as farmers everyone was largely self-sufficient; and partly too because life was simpler, nobody cooked according to recipes with exotic ingredients; no miracle cleaning scrub or washproduct formula substituted for elbow grease; no frozen TV dinners took the place of a home-cooked meal. Consequently, grandma carried mostly basic staples like flour, sugar, soap, oil, beer, coffee and interestingly, the daily bread and rolls which were delivered fresh each morning by a young man on his bicycle.

But there were also non-essentials, the stuff of interest to us kids: Jars of hard candy with Murano glass designs, Schleckstengel (lollipops), licorice shoelaces, chocolate bars like Toblerone, and on weekends, pastry. Cream-laden squishy Napoleons or eclairs for twenty centimes (5 cents U.S. then), and the dry macaroons or pigs ears for half that price. Grandma carried an assortment of cigarettes for men (women did not yet smoke, unless it was a pipe) each accompanied by a book of matches. One could buy cigarettes singly as well, just like cigars.

Most of the store's inventory, aside from the hard candy, was prepackaged: The cube sugar in a carton, the coffee and chicory in white and blue striped bags, fruits and vegetables in cans of course, the spaghetti in paper and the blueing in small gauze bags. The soup cubes (super large bouillon cubes) were perhaps the only ready mix food. No Muesli from the box—the Swiss hardly would eat this preparation designed by a vegetarian clinic to cure stomach ulcers, for breakfast. It was a main meal, if we ever had it, prepared from scratch with oatmeal,

apples, condensed milk, hazelnuts and some lemon juice.

There was little measuring and weighing involved in Grandma's sales. The scales on the countertop with the shiny copper bowl, the black and golden weights were more of a symbolic item . . . but we loved to play with it.

The small store would never have passed today's health department inspections. Dusty cobwebs hung in the corners—flypapers were black with victims. However, the mice were taken care of by a bevy of cats. Periodically there were puddles of water near the chest filled with chunks of rectangular ice blocks. An old type refrigerator for a few bottles of beer and orangina. A few posters were tacked on the wall, and as in most establishments during the war, a framed photo of Henri Guisan, the Swiss Chief of the Army, stayed up there long after his colors had faded.

Business was rarely brisk, but it kept Grandma abreast of local happenings. In order to gain access to the store, she had to be summoned by a shrill doorbell which could be heard in the chicken yard as well. She then appeared, leisurely, with a huge key to unlock the door. Shoppers could wait on a bench if she was delayed, and many women were happy to rest a few minutes. The dealing over, also a social occasion, Grandma returned to her quarters, took off her black shawl and continued knitting one of the 24 pair of black socks she presented to the male members of the family each Christmas. (By the way, she often shared the living room, not the "gute Stube" (parlor), with grandpa's sick hens, cooped up in a box, or in the spring with whole flats of hatchlings needing the extra warmth behind the green tiled stove. While we were amused by the birds' antics, we sure did not appreciate their smell.)

On our visits to Grandma's house we could hardly wait for that bell to chatter. She entrusted us with the key, and did we not feel important, unlocking that door! Actually we had an agenda: We always hoped, that once the customer had left, she would take pity on us and decide that one of the pastries was too old or damaged to sell. We gladly devoured her loss. Only when I absolved my compulsory "Landarbeit" (students working on farms during the war as substitutes for the soldiers guarding the borders) did I realize that her store operated mostly in the red and was subsidized by the chicken and egg business. Grandma was liberal at giving credit and bad at collecting debts. There were no adding machines; prices were pencilled on the wrapping paper and added twice, once up, once down, to insure against mistakes; change was calculated in the head; the money kept in a cigar box inside a deep drawer of the counter. Many people, especially if they also sent their children, even tots with a shopping list, had their debts registered in a blue booklet and were supposed to pay at the end of the month. Obviously, some did not.

No matter what age, everyone brought a basket or string bag for carrying the purchase back home. And nobody ever touched any merchandise before having paid for it. This taboo was strictly enforced by the parents. Furthermore, and these rules applied everywhere, you only entered a store with the intention of buying something. You window-shopped instead of browsed. Even in the department store a saleslady would offer her help if you looked at something for more than an instant. Most of us were embarrassed to say that we were only looking; we often bought something we really did not intend to.

So, whenever Grandma's bell rang, she was assured of a sale, even only five centimes' worth of candy. Tending to this store was her only exercise, yet she was over 80 when she died.

# Fahrt ins Blaue
# Overland (Into the Blue) Excursion

Our family never afilliated with one of those societies the Swiss were traditionally fond of: Neither choral group nor "Jass" (card) club; neither ski club nor folkloric society. Father may have been a member of the Touring Club (an equivalent of AAA), not for the social functions, however, but to have trips to other countries facilitated and to get road assistance should his car break down. PTA as such was nonexistent. Mother might have attended an "Eltereabig" (parent night) at the beginning of the school year to make the acquaintance of the teacher.

My brother finally broke ranks when he joined the cub scouts, got to wear a uniform, spend Sundays away from the family and go camping.

On our solitary Sunday drives, prior to the big war, we regularly encountered busloads of club members (who usually had no prior knowledge of where they would end up), in some well-known excursion spot (Uusflugspunkt). After they had oriented themselves, stretched their legs and perhaps assembled to play or sing some music to an appreciative village audience, they invariably headed for their true destination: A renowned restaurant famous for its Mistchratzerli (Literally: Dungheap scratcher, or young chicken) and blue trout with its mouth agape. Depending on the season or the cycle of slaughtering, they might have feasted on a Puureplatte (farmer's plate) of sausage, ham, bacon, wädli (boiled knuckles of the pig), perhaps with sauerkraut and boiled potatoes. Dessert usually was a meringue with mountains of rich whipped cream, followed by a café Schnapps (cherry brandy) to help the digestion. The jovial ambiance, the laughter, the joking, the backslapping was considerably abetted by glasses of red wine, mostly of local vintage. Clouds of cigar and pipe smoke circled the low ceilings. At some point, though, there was a clanking on a glass. All quieted down for a speech or two, followed by some singing, a yodel solo or some dancing to Ländlermusik (country music) with the dominant strain of the accordion.

These outings were not designed to be educational; they were frankly geared to spending some club dues on good victuals and comradery, a chance for the women (or husbands) to emerge, get dressed up or wear a national costume. To have fun.

# Wösch
# Laundry

My mother, too, washed every week. But only socks, and in winter an occasional woolen sweater. The bulk of the laundry was done only every four to six weeks in a special room, the Wöschchuchi (wash kitchen), down in the basement. Even by that time the piles were not humongous since clothes were changed only once a week, on Sunday, after the Saturday bath. Sheets were changed before laundry day but aired every non-rainy day hanging over the bedroom windowsill.

Why Monday was the traditional day for laundry, I don't know. Unless it had to do with that Sunday change business. Or, if the weather interfered with the drying process, you could still have your wash back in the closet or drawers by the following weekend. Still to this day with automatic dryers, laundromats seem busier on Mondays than the rest of the week.

Whatever the reason, the normal daily routine was suspended on laundry Monday. Mother got up before six a.m. to fill a huge kettle with cold water and light a fire under it to heat it up. The white items like sheets or father's shirts, or our underwear were later boiled (koched) in this cauldron; and some of its hot water sloshed into zinc-lined tubs for the rest of the dirty clothes.

Our mother did not do the actual washing herself, but hired a laundress to do the heavy work. The date of the laundry day was immutable not just because of the schedule for the whole apartment house, but the woman also had a full schedule for weeks ahead if she did good work. No wonder, mother kept an anxious eye out for weather indicators—since except for personal barometers (arthritis included), there were no official weather reports.

No matter which Frau . . . (their names changed frequently, you can carry on as laundress only so long ) appeared around seven a.m., she followed pretty much the same ritual: Changed into old clothes, put on an oil cloth or rubber apron and large rubber boots, drained the soak water from the tubs by pulling out the wooden stopper (a drain in the middle of the floor swallowed the gushing water into the sewer), ladled a few buckets full of the now hot water onto the presoaked items, dumped soapflakes into the kettle and drowned the whites in the boiling water, started soaping everything else on a washboard with a huge cube of brown soap, periodically stirred the kettle with a huge wooden paddle, wrung everything out by hand before rinsing in a second tub, did it again after rinsing, before she loaded the stuff into a mechanical centrifugal wringer powered by water.

Perhaps this wringing everything, including the sheets, contributed to the exhaustion of the women and the reason why we got to meet a whole slew of them over time.

Nine o'clock meant a Znüni break, a mid-morning snack of hearty fare, bread, cheese, Wurst, and coffee, which was to sustain the woman's energy.

Towards eleven, just before mother began preparing the main meal of the day, the first batch of laundry, primarily sheets (which took the longest to dry) was ready in a wicker basket to be hung up. The clotheslines were in the small, gravelly backyard, strung from hooks attached to two opposing goal posts on which carpets were beaten on off days and from which hung the neighborhood "monkeys" after school.

The women never ate lunch at our table but separately in the kitchen. I always wondered why, but never asked. Did they feel embarrassed in their work clothes with their lobster red, swollen hands to be seen by the man of the house? Or was it class distinction? The lack of contact between them and us always seemed very deliberate.

Toward 3:30 p.m. a sweet afternoon snack was served, once more in the Wöschchuchi. By that time, the women were probably attending to the most delicate of items and began cleaning up all the equipment, the tubs, the washboard, the kettle. They even removed the ashes from the cauldron and scrubbed the cement floor of the laundry.

Meanwhile mother had checked all day long on the drying progress of the clothes on the line; took down the dry and folded; called the kids to help with the sheets; pinned up wet loads; scolded children playing too close to the clean wash; toted baskets to the apartment—and generally had a hectic day. Saint Peter (he's traditionally in charge of weather in Swiss folklore) could create a big problem if he produced rain on laundry day. Unless there was a special drying room set aside in the attic, the day's laundry had to be hung in the basement. It was damp and the drying process would take longer . . . also the clothes would not smell as sweet. But at least, the pile would be out of the way until the ironing lady, in our case Frau Bräm, arrived two or three days later to flatten wrinkles out of everything (even bathtowels). She did this on the kitchen table, upholstered for the day with blankets and an old sheet. Our Frau Bräm must have been a grandmother—and I always wished she was mine, such a soothing influence she brought to our house. Since irons did not generate steam, nor had temperature settings, she sprinkled everything which had been so laboriously dried with warm water and rolled it into tight wads before wielding her iron.

I don't think there was much aside from a drawer or armoire full of ironed, neatly piled clothes, especially frilly nightgowns that could evoke as much pride and satisfaction from a Swiss Hausfrau. While you had to rely on others' judgment about your abilities as a cook beautifully arranged closets and drawers gave instantaneous positive feedback.

I temporarily caught this fever the day when I was finally allowed to iron a few handkerchiefs under Frau Bräm's tutelage: No rolled hems, no asymmetrical corners, all stacked facing the same way. Kleenex were not invented yet, so there were always tons of snow-white handkerchiefs for men and smaller, fancy edged ones for ladies. A clean handkerchief was a prerequisite for our leaving the house each morning.

By the way, neither laundress nor Frau Bräm made more than twenty dollars plus carfare for their day's labor. My mother reputedly paid well (and usually had some goodies for them to take home).

# Metzgerei
# Butchershop

When I was a girl, a typical Swiss housewife straightened her apartment each day, turned the mattresses and made the beds with sheets, pillows and featherbed freshly aired on the bedroom windowsill, before she began her daily morning rounds of at least three stores: The baker, the butcher and the grocer. A fourth, the Milchlade (milk store) was added if she had missed the milkman who passed by the house early every day, or if she needed cheese.

Compared to the other stores, the butchershop always seemed intimidatingly sanitized: Tiled in white with sparkling glass display cases to protect the meat from wandering hands or airborne germs; large wooden chopping blocks scoured or shaved every day; butchers in white uniforms with a white apron on top. (sometimes with traces of red), wielding large knives and honing them before filling every new order;  salesladies also wrapped in white aprons, with white oversleeves up to their elbows. But no gloves. Plastic had yet to be developed, just like electric refrigeration.

No saranwrap—no precut portions of anything wrapped in plastic. But where pork chops, steaks and roasts come from was unmistakably evident. Pieces of animal carcasses dangled on meathooks from the ceiling. Pigs' heads and knuckles nestled among bundles of fresh parsley behind the glass. There displayed were these loopy brains, tight kidneys, squishy lungs and feathery tripe, sides of ribs and bacon, oxtails and pale, rough tongues, and pans of blood sausage. A veritable anatomy lesson: Bones for dogs, marrow bones for the pot roast.

Everything was cut, ground, pounded and trimmed to order. If a special demand could not be filled from the display at hand, the butcher disappeared through a heavily insulated wooden door into the cold storage chamber. He returned more than likely with the desired item. As a rule, chickens had to be ordered specially in advance. Somehow they either had to lay eggs until they were too old or happened to be roosters. The latter turned into crispy fried poulets, a special weekend treat with pommes frites—while the hens ended up in the stew pot.  Lamb was uncommon.

During the war horse meat became popular; I believe it was not rationed or sold at half coupon. But sold in special stores only less camouflaged: you can sell salami anywhere!

Hard, soft, black, white or brown sausages, fresh, smoked or air-dried coldcuts were sold from a counter separate from the bloody meat. Usually the butcher's wife's domain, a woman's in any case, she always had a Rugeli Wurst (a round of sausage) ready for the children, who always had to act as if they did not really want it, but they were happy if she insisted. Besides cutting things to order by hand or the slicing machine, she functioned as cashier for the whole shop. Handling money and meat simultaneously did not seem to pose a problem then. If the butcher had to tend to the register himself, he merely wiped his hands on his apron before and after the cash transaction, and then waited on the next customer without further ado. After all, the meat was going to be cooked.

On certain days of the week, depending on the season, you could and still can, buy traditional specialties, such as blood and liver sausage, adrio, wädli (boiled knuckles) and gsottnigs (corned beef) with sauerkraut. By the way, the butcher was not the only one who cut down on cooking time for customers. Grocers sold boiled potatoes for rösti (home fries) and beets for salad.

Butchers, like bakers, did a lot of preparing behind the scenes, like making bratwurst and cervelat (knockwurst), and of course the Wieners aka (hot dogs), while normal people still slept. To catch up on their rest, their establishment was closed between noon and three p.m. Today butchers are losing their business to the one-stop supermarkets which get their inventory prepared from large production plants. Their workers keep regular working hours, and meat is available all day long until closing time at 6:30 p.m., except for Thursdays, when closing time is moved up to 8 p.m.

My grandfather was a well-known butcher before he filled a market niche with his chicken farm. Even though he owned one of the first cars in Zürich, he had my father deliver meat and sausages on a bicycle. He pedaled the wares on his back in a huge basket. But not for long: He could not cope with all the dogs following the scent of his cargo, nipping at his legs to get to the treats. Grandma took pity on him and assigned the task to an older, stronger brother. Women could not vote in those days—but they carried clout in the domestic sphere.

By the way, you would never have found a man shopping for food; for his own Znüni, a wurst, a roll and a bottle of beer, maybe. They would not be seen carrying a basket, nor later, a paperbag full of groceries. All their purchases had to be decoyed in packpapier (brown paper) secured with twine. Except for the butcher, no grocer was equipped for such amenities. You bagged your own order in a basket or stringbag; apples, onions, tomatoes, were loose before small paper bags came along. And you still do your own bagging the same way today, unless you buy a large bag from the cashier and with the changing times and equality of the sexes, even some men now do the marketing.

But in those earlier days only the wife was known by name in the stores, since she alone appeared almost daily or sent her kids, even preschoolers. Fridays might have been skipped in favor of getting a piece of fish from the market or making a Wähe (a rectangular fruit tart with loads of custard) as a substitute on the traditionally meatless day. Saturday was the only day when people shopped for two days in a row.

# Chrank Sii (Being Sick)

**B**eing sick was also different.

To have a cold, for example, meant sitting under a towel over a steaming kettle of hot water infused with chamomile or eucalyptus oil, gargling with salt or hydrogen peroxide, sucking on pea-sized and pea-green rubbery eucalyptus drops to keep the sinuses open and to definitely drink what seemed to be gallons of herbal teas, licorice, Icelandic moss . . . all sweetened with honey or dark Kandiszucker (rock candy).

The immigration officer in Hoboken opened the metal box containing my assortment of the most essential herbs and wondered, "Are you a witch doctor?" No, I was merely going to continue the lessons inculcated by mother via generations of wisdom. According to this legacy I also knew what to do in case of nosebleeds and hiccups to which we kids seemed to fall victim frequently.

To have a temperature, however, was yet another cup of teas, literally. Additionally, you definitely repaired to bed and stayed there until the thermometer, pressed under your arm or stuck in one of two other openings in your body (one requiring Vaseline) declared you "normal." Until the quicksilver fell to that point, your calves were wrapped with cool vinegar wickel (compresses) or cool, wet washcloths dried out on your forehead. If your cough was raspy, your chest was slathered with some kind of hot grease—either dog, marmot or goose—and covered with an itchy, woolen piece of fabric, secured by huge safety pins. This same piece of fabric at another time might hug a poultice of fried onions to your chest.

Blattere (chicken pox), Masere (measles) were in Dr. Ma's competence unless she suspected Scharlach (scarlet fever). In that case as well as Chüüchhuschte (whooping cough), (especially if one's breath became short), or a tender to the touch stomachache, the family doctor was summoned pronto. I haven't heard much about diphtheria or appendicitis recently, but they were frequent topics when I grew up. Incisions were like badges of honor to be compared for length. Nobody wanted my tonsils (no ice cream treatment either!), so I don't know about hospitals. But as a one-time visitor, I was duly impressed by the quiet efficiency of serene faced deaconesses in blue frocks, white or black aprons and starched headdresses.

Dr. Zbinden always appeared promptly in his small black car or on the tram during the war. While he was anticipated, the sickroom was aired, we got washed and combed, stuck in clean pajamas and the linen might even have been changed. A place for his overcoat and hat

*From Here To There*

was cleared on the Garderobe (coat rack). A clean towel and fresh soap were laid out in the bathroom—even though he always preferred the kitchen for his ablution. His diagnosis, delivered calmly, affected most likely a goodly part of the cure. We generally felt better the moment he replaced the spoon (which had served as a tongue depressor) on the saucer which mother was holding, and folded the stethoscope back into the classic black bag. Predictably he would prescribe more tea and perhaps some homeopathic pillules or drops of some kind based on natural ingredients, which now would be termed "alternative" remedies. Like most doctors of the time, Dr. Zbinden believed that the fever would help the healing process. Sometimes the temperature got even turned up a notch with Antiphlogestin wraps or (Heaven forbid) a mustard plaster.

If we presented a puzzle or a severe case, the doctor would stop in again the following day. But no matter what we were suffering from, he was the arbiter as to when we might get up and back to school again. During the compulsory period of recuperation between getting out of bed and back to school, we had to take a few walks in fresh air first and swallow some tonic, either from the pharmacy or a grandmother's medicine cabinet. Ours specialized in elderberry syrup.

For non acute illnesses the doctor also had afternoon walk-in hours . . . no appointments accepted. The wait could be interminably long. What did the patients suffer from? The names of their afflictions have probably changed by now anyway. Chräbs (cancer) was a tumor (Gschwür), Rheumatisch or Häxeschuss (sciatica) are most likely subdivided into more precise diagnoses.

In retrospect there seemed to be a bias against chemical compounds put out by the pharmaceutical giants in Basel that had only recently switched over from manufacturing paint. But I recall the more fashionable ladies popping aspirins for pain and headache brought on by the Föhn, a warm wind from the south, which makes the Alps appear near and clear to the delight of tourists and their cameras. (Dr. Zbinden would have advised the ladies that strong black coffee and lemon juice accomplishes the same results.)

He, like many others, believed in the motto "different life, not better pills" which advocated proper diet, fresh air, light and water as a means of taking responsibility for one's health. We tried our best.

My father, for example, took every opportunity to shed his shoes and socks, roll up his pants and tramp through dewy grass according to the preachings of Dr. Kneipp. Was this doc responsible for all those hot Fuessbäder (foot baths) in wet, cold weather?

My mother preferred the healing properties of the hot mineral springs of Baden. There she soaked in "bathtubs" which looked as if the Roman discoverers had themselves hewn them out of the hillsides.

Were we admonished to "Wäsch d' Händ" before each meal due to a fear of bacteria, or simply to get rid of the grime and to satisfy the rules of etiquette? A moot question. But even in a restaurant, before we touched any morsel of food, off to the bathroom we marched to wash our hands and then to dry them . . . ! on a wet towel, which had been used by umpteen people before, unless it was one of those roll-up jobs on which you might manage to find a dry spot. And why did we only drink mineral water, Elmer Citro or Eptinger instead of tap water? Was there a dim memory of infamously poisoned water? After all, we slurped it at public fountains right from the spout, but never from the heavy metal cup attached with a chain if an adult was close—more admonition about "unsanitary" stuff.

Even as babies we were aired every day and in any weather in substantial prams until we graduated into Sportswäge (low, sit-up carriages). As toddlers we played in the nearest park, and once in school we were let loose on the neighborhood until suppertime. Sickly kids like myself spent months in a Kinderheim up in the mountains surrounded by woods or fields to gain strength. To alleviate the suffering of saying repeated goodbyes, parental visits were discouraged, but packages were encouraged, though we had to share their contents under the watchful control of a "Tante" (aunt). Tüüfschnuufe (deep breathing) still rings in my ears when I find myself among evergreens. Aromatherapy?

Novels have been written about TB sufferers seeking a cure in the rarified air of Davos. And for a while rides in old-fashioned airplanes were prescribed for severe whooping cough. But the air today isn't what it used to be!

When it comes to light, we might have overdone it, probably in part due to a change in aesthetics: The TAN came in. Sunbathing now tints the previously coveted white faces of ladies and red cheeks of children. And pretty soon the tan migrated all over the body—with sometimes painful results. Vacation success was often judged by the shade of the "bruun" (brown), whereas previously the quantity of food had been the criterion.

Aside from Dr. Bircher and his Müsli there were no diet gurus with any influence that I am aware of. We always ate lots of apples, Huut und Pütschgi (skin and core). At least we were not obese, perhaps not even chubby enough for grandparents who invariably felt an obligation to fatten us up. Iss mein Kind! (Eat my child!) The success of my children's stay in Switzerland was always measured by the scales.

Grown ups seemed to consume quite a few "Bitters" or Schnapps after meals to help digestion. We might be given a cube of sugar doused with Melissengeist or Dr. Zeller's Balsam for an occasional upset.

Some measure of prevention we would have liked to see forgotten—like the clove of garlic on a string around our neck. Thank goodness we were spared from walking with sliced onions in our shoes, one of my grandfather's practices. And then there was this Norwegian cod liver oil—even with lemon juice the mere smell made me wretch.

Once in this country I began to neglect my box of herbs for the fast-acting pills and shots and vitamins. No more time to be sick the Swiss way. But now I watch bemusedly the Western world return to "witch doctor" ways, or at least to acknowledge their legitimacy. Of course remedies now come in convenient forms of salves, wraps, drops, bandages and even tea bags! But you still have to brew the tea, even if you can heat the water in a microwave and simply dunk the bag. I still use a Nägeli (clove) to dull a toothache.

Perhaps even bed rest will be "in" again some time. Shouldn't be onerous with a portable radio, television and a cell phone—all gadgets non-existent in my time. So what did we do? Daydream? Read the one or two books we owned over again? Memorize the Pestalozzikalender? Draw with Caran d'Ache color pencils? Project silhouettes with our hands onto a wall? Or just simply sleep and enjoy being served in bed until we got tired of the Habersuppe (oatmeal soup) and grated apples diet, which was a sign we were on the mend.

# Getting Around Town

If you weren't inclined to walk (unlikely as this was in my young days), or your destination was a bit too far away, you could always board one of those blue trams with the white Zürileu coat of arms, or a bus. They delivered you to the zoo or to an elegant café in town, to the train station or to the university. Even though we lived two kilometers from my school, and this distance had to be traversed four times most days, I personally used the convenience of tram number 3 only when it poured. (Since my parents did not quite approve of my going for higher education, I tried to cut expenses wherever possible.)

On those rainy days it was standing room only for young people since we always gave up our seat to people who looked older. Seats were uncomfortable anyway, hard, slatted wooden benches along the windows. Dripping umbrellas caused little rivers to flow between the ridges of the wooden floors, constructed like doormats which scrape the dirt from your shoes. Depending on the distance that we rode, a conductor sold us tickets, white, blue or orange and marked the stop and where we might have to change lines on the printed city transportation net with a Löchlizange. Like checks, he carried these tickets inserted into a leather satchel which was attached to a shoulder belt.

Wherever trolley lines coming from different parts of the city crossed, and people changed cars or buses, major hubs of activities developed. The closest one to our house was the Stauffacher, named after one of those mythological founders of the Swiss confederation. The actual heart of the location is St. Jacob's Church, its steeple an exclamation point in Zürich's skyline. In the middle ages, the lepers were banished to these grounds, across the river Sihl, then the city boundary. St. Jacob's is built on the site of the chapel which was their refuge.

Stauffacher offers everything a small village might. Restaurants (these days even a McDonalds and Kentucky Fried Chicken), banks, shoe and clothing stores, a Swiss knife and watch boutique, an antique book seller, a chain grocery and much more, including a movie house. They have taken on more importance in daily life than the time chiming church with the large clock face. Specially since its magnificent landmark magnolia trees, their blossoms always definitive proof to a gray city that spring indeed had sprung . . . gave way to glass shelters for computerized ticket automats. Instead of also merely protecting waiting passengers from the elements they have attracted substance abusers of all kind to loiter there between police raids.

In the 30's and 40's hubs such as the Stauffacher were ideal locations for selling newspapers, the only source of information aside

from the radio. The hawkers were older men and women, rarely boys. Vieing for sales, they announced important headlines as titillatingly as possible on placards stuck in a headband or worn on their back or chest, or both. Some of these vendors were known all over town for their idiosyncratic style—especially when peddling special editions informing about the progress of the war with their "Extrablatt . . . extra . . ."

If you could not find your preferred paper, mostly party-linked, on the street, you could always find an issue at a nearby kiosk, or in the reeking tobacco store which also sold lottery tickets.

My favorite, albeit seasonal (fall and winter) enterprises were Heissi Marroni huts (roasted chestnut stands). Typically they were operated by Italians (or Swiss from the Ticino) since the south is where chestnuts are cultivated. We always got a kick out of how they garbled Swiss German. They were especially fond of small bambinis and slipped many a hot chestnut into their coat pockets for warming little hands. Though they were standing in front of two charcoal heated pans, one to roast and one to keep the chestnuts warm under wet burlap bags, they were wrapped in umpteen layers of colorful clothes and shawls, weighing their wares with gloves, (that looked like modern driving gloves) into newspaper rolled up pastry-bag fashion.

Of course, bicycles were an alternative to walking or using public transportation. Many businesses and even schools and governmental offices offered bike parking racks in front of their buildings. I graduated to this level of mobility when my father traded a camera for a bike. It was equipped with skinny racing tires (canvas with a thin layer of rubber as profile). They were prone to get stuck in trolley tracks and picked up the smallest puncturing items. Supposedly there were no traditional rubber tires available during the war, and besides (so the rationalization) racing tires reduced the weight of the bike I had to pedal up some stretch of the Züriberg, where my school was located.

Nowadays of course, the city abounds with cars, causing traffic jams and pollution. Policemen have been replaced by traffic lights. As have the ticket selling trolley conductors by the machines at every stop. Instead a controller may periodically mingle plainclothed among the passengers asking for a show of valid tickets. Riding "black" results in a hefty fine; but some passengers consider the dare worthwhile in the long run since controls occur rather infrequently. Women are among the motormen but young people and children no longer cede their seats to their elders. With the arrival of sex equality hardly a chivalrous man can be found to stand up for a woman.

The marroni roasters are still there, but without a wooden protective hut. Yet the aroma of roasted chestnuts still permeates the air during the gray months of the city.

Oschter haas

Glücks säuli
marzipan

Glücks chäfer

öpfel im Schlofrok

Läbchueche
GEBURTS TAG

3königschranz

Prüssli

Birrewegge

Mohrechopf

Zimmetstärn

Praline's
Lindt

Berliner

SPANISCH BRÖTLI BAHN

Schräbeli

Püürli

Japonais

Bäretatse

Müüsli

Tirggel

Cremeschnitte

Meringue

Spitzbueb

Marzipan

Charlotte Russe

Cornet

Zopf

Weggli

Pfünderli

Grittibänz

not to scale!

# Beckerei . . . Konditorei . . .

"Did you ever bake?" Debbie asked.

I had mentioned Mailänderli, Gugelhopf and lastly Stollen, so I figured I had exhausted the topic. During sleepless nights thoughts sometimes began to float in all directions like groping tentacles of Tintenfisch (octopus).

So, it began to dawn on me that Switzerland really had, and still has, a very different "baking culture" from the U.S. To wit: Here a hostess honors guests with muffins, home-baked rolls or, at the very least, warm bread at dinner; and serves whenever possible a homemade pie or cake for dessert or coffee. In Switzerland, if we entertained at home, a rare enough occasion, we never even served cold bread at a cooked meal. Perhaps that is why we gorged on bread and butter in the restaurant while waiting for the main course despite parental warnings "verdirbsch dä Appetit" (you'll spoil your appetite), and the fact that each cold slice might have cost extra. Instead of baking a dessert as the pièce de résistance, we bought an assortment of pâtisserie (pastries) or a fancy torte from the best baker we knew.

There were always several in the vicinity. They all sold bread but each seemed to have his strength and weakness in the other departments. We bought from each what we considered, according to our tastebuds, his specialty. Thus some bakers were really confiseurs, excelling in working with chocolate: Creating pralines (cream-filled chocolates and truffles); chocolate critters according to the seasons: cream-filled mice complete with tails for Christmas; Easterbunnies in many stances and sizes (and nougat eggs); ladybugs wrapped in red foil with black dots, replete with a set of black paper legs; marzipan fruit (and pigs for good luck at New Year's) . . . Others made unforgettable Konfekt (cookies) while others were preferred for their bread and Wähe. And then there were the pastry chefs . . .

Whenever I was sent to buy bread and pastry at the same time, I was confronted with the dilemma of whether to make two trips or how to hide the first purchase from the next baker so as not to reveal a partiality. This problem is now largely solved since the neighborhood supermarket carries everything under one roof (and in the freezer as well) and tastes have become less discriminating. Besides, the number of bakers has shrunk considerably; not just due to the time-saving convenience of the one-stop market. But also because fewer young people are willing to get up at an ungodly hour in order to 1) have fresh bread—Weggli (a flat roll, buttery, with two humps)—and Gipfel (croissant) ready for the breakfast table at 7 a.m.; 2) finish the Püürli (4 hand-sized crusty loaves of bread baked together in the shape of a four leaf clover or "Schild") to be consumed with Wurst or Chääs zum Znüüni (9 o'clock snack); 3) bring up, at least on Fridays, the Wähe, tarts filled with fruit of the season (apples perennially, sliced or grated) or cheese by 10 o'clock; and lastly 4) arrange the Guetzli and Torten. This succession of goodies, adapted to the rhythm of the day, was probably carved in stone. A baker's day may have been done by 11 in the morning.

Walking into a Swiss bakery for the first time can be an overwhelming experience for somebody, young or old, who hesitates making decisions. Die Qual der Wahl. (The torture of choice.) How to select from 20 some pastries and tortes? I personally decided against anything with colored glaze or too much cream as being vulgar. After a short period of experimentation most people, however, seem to settle down to their favorites. Ordering becomes routine, which even the baker's wife behind the counter can in time anticipate. Depending on the season there may be slight variations in the fruit tartlets or additions like Vermicelle (little worms of chestnut puree) in winter.

The most seductive selection of pastry was usually available on Saturday—for Sunday treats I suppose. On that day we always had ours in a café after a walk or drive somewhere else. But no matter where somewhere else was, there we beamed in on the same café we always frequented. This tradition filtered down to my children. One day in Schwyz my brother asked Hester, "Have you ever seen the Bundesbrief?" "No," was her answer, "but I can show you the way to your traditional coffeeshop." And as the establishment was traditional, so was our choice of pastry from their particular offering.

Our family was spoilt inasmuch as we had Guetzli with coffee after the fruit dessert of the midday main meal even during the week. Except during the war of course.

There was a distinction, however. The weekday pastries were cheaper by half, drier and would keep in the porcelain box—hazelnut or coconut macaroons, Prüüsli (pigs ears), Spitzbuebe (rascals, butter cookies with chocolate covered ends), Bääretatse (bear paws), and Schoggi S (chocolate meringue in the form of, naturally, an S) . . .

The Sunday selection, on the other hand, was made from the expensive and in a sense international repertoire: Japonais, Charlotte Russe, Napoleons, Mohrenchopf (Moor's head), Vermicelle, meringue with mountains of whipped cream, Berliner . . . My mother preceded the rich Guetzli whenever possible with a butter croissant and topped her enjoyment of her Zvieri (4 o'clock repast) with her weekly cigarette, a habit many ladies had started to adopt to declare their emancipation. We kids used to speculate about people's character and station in life by the pastry they ate. How else could we entertain ourselves while having to sit through the coffee hour?

The Zvieri rite was and still is (dietary considerations notwithstanding) part of the Swiss lifestyle. Comes 4 o'clock, cafés, even during the week, are chockfull of ladies (and some gentlemen, now that the older male generation is not afraid to enjoy genteel leisure) who indulge in their favorite treat with a Schale Gold (milk coffee). (By the way, there are no free refills.) Frankly, some of us girls were secretly looking forward to our future life (married, of course) when we would shed our morning apron and leave the household behind (under pretext of doing some errand, naturally). With the growing AHV (social security) population this café culture is not likely to disappear. Can you imagine though, the deprivation Switzerland experienced during WWII with sporadic coffee imports? This beverage, which traditionally accompanied every meal, was stretched with dried chicory, turnips and even ground-up acorns. Real, strong coffee was reserved for festive occasions or the rare visitor.

If you were at work you probably still enjoyed this coffeebreak. As many other older ladies, one of my distant relatives was employed by a small firm to brew and serve coffee in the morning and coffee with crumpets in the afternoon. She knew exactly how many lumps of sugar or how much milk everybody in her charge desired. Her popularity was measured in tips and Christmas presents. Now, was the job created because coffee machines were not yet invented, was the secretary's job too valuable, or did the secretary refuse?

There were, of course, still some homemade goodies, though you might find them at the baker's as well. Chances are that some grandmother still baked Birrewegge oder Birrebrot, a paste of dried pears, prunes and perhaps figs wrapped in a bread-like dough. This goodie seemed to go out of style—who still dried pears? Öpfelchrapfe oder Öpfel im Schlafrock (nightshirt), both apples baked whole, and Öpfel Strudel were more likely still prepared at home with the help of "we make it—you bake it" pâte brisé dough pieces, which I remember buying from the baker by the pound long before they ended up in stores or appeared in the U.S. where we still don't have ready-made Paschtetli (puff pastry shells), which could be filled up for a quick Sunday meal.

Depending on where our grandmothers were born they might also have had regional treasures among their recipes based on local ingredients. Being German my paternal Oma stuck to Stollen and Berliner. My maternal granny was from Bally shoe country (Aargau) and made Bölle (onion) and Chruut mit Späckwürfeli (chard with bacon bits), Wähe, Müüslibletter (sage leaf) fritters for lunch as well as Mailänderli (sugar cookies), Zimmetstärn (cinnamon stars), and Chräbbeli (anise seed cookies, toothbreakers) for Christmas. She also fried Schänkeli (a thigh-shaped, dense doughnut). Starved for some pastry I ventured a batch one day in the bush of the Cameroons. By chance a visitor from Basel dropped in—we made short shrift of this Heiweh (homesick) goodie despite the looming possibility of a very heavy stomach. I saved his offering of Basler Leckerli (another honey cookie) for a future craving.

Then there was Tante Friedel who kept alive the tradition of Chnüüschiibe (patellas) alias Fasnachtschüechli (carnival cookie) from an elastic dough which we stretched over our knee until we could read through it. The Blätz (patch) were fried golden in an oil bath. Since they were much larger than the pan, they came out with plenty of nooks and crannies for confectioner's sugar.

The very traditional Läbchueche (spiced honey cake) and Biber, often filled with almond paste, are left in the hands of the baker as is the bread, with perhaps the exception of the Zopf (braid, a type of hallah). I vaguely remember trying my hand at one for Christmas after taking the compulsory cooking course. This attempt was much to my mother's consternation, who, I'm sure, bought a backup from the baker. Originally Zopf, artfully woven with up to 9 strands, was for Christmas, but nowadays it is served for Sunday breakfast as well.

The ordinary bread was purchased fresh every day from the baker. No wonder our family had lots of stale heels and slices to feed the swans and gulls at the lake, or to augment the farmer wife's rabbit food. But sometimes the leftovers were fried with apples as Vogelheu (bird's hay) for supper or converted into an Uuflauf (a custard-like quiche with fruit or cheese) for Friday's lunch. Möcke (morsels) could also be floated in the much beloved soup or in coffee together with a hunk of butter. There were special dishes—Chacheli—cereal type bowls with higher walls to accommodate the plentiful liquid.

The bread assortment in the city was fairly unimaginative: Long loaves (Pfünderli, Zweipfünder—one or two pounders) or St. Galler (boule): Wiis, halbruuch or ruuch (white, half-white or whole wheat—but not as dark as pumpernickel). The baker or the help always asked "hell oder dunkel?" (light-brown or well-baked) before they wrapped the bread in tissue paper. There may have been one or two more varieties, but nothing like you encounter on the shelves these days, even a ring from the Valais, baked once a year hung from the rafters and soaked before eating, or so I am told. What is more surprising is that people who pooh-poohed "eating for health" just a few years ago (like my grandmother who said, "I have watched pots all my life, but I have never seen a vitamin.") are now buying big into the trend as exemplified by the proliferation of bread recipes. Thank goodness Americans too believe in the healthier trend—it was difficult to get used to the foam rubbery type of Wonderbread. I would drive miles to German delis to find some crusty bread. And why was there sugar in bread with which you made meat sandwiches?

The Grittibänz for Santa Claus and the drei Königschranz (three kings' wreath) for January are still traditional Christmas bread items. But the one that spells Christmas for me is the Tirggel (even though it is now available year round). A Tirggel can be any shape—round and small to hang on the tree or, theoretically, as large as a cookie sheet. It is a woodcut-like picture cake, flat and very thin, brown on top and light on the underside. It is hard but dissolves on your tongue. It can depict historical events, fish, swaddled kids, trades, fertility symbols or it can even be a wedding announcement. Few households would attempt making these little works of art at home, unless merely to replicate the unadorned cookies. The old molds for the Tirggel have by now ended up in museums, but I would call a few my own if I had followed my instincts for folk art and had sacrificed my meager pocket money way back when.

The Tirggel embodies baking culture. The earliest earthen molds and recipes stem from 4000 years ago. They were found in Egypt and Mesopotamia. From there, some historians suggest, the Romans spread the confection over their realm. Since it is made with flour and honey and mixed with exotic spices (ginger, cinnamon and anise) plus rosewater, some others suspect the Venetians to be the Tirggel's PR men since they had an interest in selling their merchandise. The Tirggel is first mentioned in the chronicles of Zürich, where it seems to have taken root primarily in the 1400's, when a "witch" was immured alive for killing her husband with a poisoned one. History also records the banning of this luxury item by puritanical city fathers. The expression "dä hät en Tirggel" (he is drunk) can be linked to it as well. Guildmembers returning home (under the influence) from their get-togethers, often brought the family a Tirggel as appeasement. Some more historians speculate it may have also served as sacrificial offering to the gods.

My appreciation of this cookie has not waned since I began to realize that it is now manufactured by machines equipped with imprinting cylinders of silicon. The number of true artisans using wood molds has diminished to less than a handful.

Mouth watering yet?

# World War II

I have made quite a few allusions to the war. Now I had better relate some of my memories. As we had little to start with by contemporary standards, it was not traumatic for us by comparison to the rest of Europe. We merely stretched what we had and made it go a little further.

While the war started officially on September 1, 1939, it had long been anticipated. As a matter of fact there was an earlier partial mobilization of the Swiss Army to protect the frontiers against a German invasion. The country experienced a wave of patriotic sentiment, abetted by the "Landi" in Zurich, a national exhibition celebrating Swiss achievement and spirit (Schweizertum) taking place every 25 years in the various regions of the country. This one stressed unity and readiness to defend Swiss neutrality to the nth degree.

But even before this, our own family had fought a kind of psychological warfare with Germany. Once when I was perhaps 8 years old my father was detained on a trip to Germany by the SS because a Hitlerjugend relative had denounced him for making anti-Nazi remarks. I know it took a lot of contraband for the boy's parents to "spring" my father, but the details of how many eggs or so were overshadowed by my terror. Similarly, my mother and I quaked in the car on Swiss soil when my father was escorted by armed guards across the border to vote on the annexation of the Sudetenland and the invasion of Austria. Because he had never fulfilled the lengthy permanent residency requirements of Zurich, we were German nationals, despite the fact that he had come to Switzerland with his parents as a teenager before World War I, spoke fluent Swiss-German and could even pronounce "Chuchichäschtli" (kitchen cabinet) with all the gutturals involved. One story has it that we became staatenlos (stateless) for a period when Dad refused to spy for the 5th column—and that Bundesrat Motta heeded my Swiss mother's pleas to facilitate the "Iichauf" (literally, buying in) or naturalization.

Of course, it had always stated "Gera, Thüringen" as my place of origin in my report card books. But having been born and bred in Zürich, I felt Swiss through and through. So, when that stuffed shirt of a Latin professor gave a speech right after the invasion of Poland, exhorting my classmates not to ostracize me due to this abomination, I began to feel really guilty and ashamed to be a foreigner, German to boot. The war took on a personal dimension.

Putting personal problems aside, there were practical things to be done during the first days of the war when the whole army was mobilized and its general elected by the government. Rationing of food and textiles was anticipated. So, the hoarding of Notrat (emergency supplies) took on serious proportions. Oil, flour, sugar and coffee flew off the shelves. My mother somehow got hold of a sack of green coffee beans, which she found and resold years after peace reigned once more. Coal was ordered. And I had to buy a pair of shoes, suitable for all occasions. Well, this pair of black brogans accompanied me, as much as I disliked them, many years of my life, through confirmation (black dress still required and borrowed from a cousin) to the decks of the New Amsterdam to sail the Atlantic, and through many years in this country, soled and resoled. The war taught me never to discard anything that could still be used or put to another function. (Recycling is my second nature.)

Rationing, when instituted, was the first tangible effect of the new reality. A whole underground network of exchanging coupons among neighbors and relatives was established. Somehow nobody was interested in the "Hülsenfrücht" (dried beans); and the bread, which now had to rest at least 24 hours on the bakers' shelves, did not taste so yummy anymore. This was probably the goal of the exercise anyway, cutting down on consumption. Or was the addition of potatoes, thereby stretching the white flour and giving the bread a sickly grey hue, the reason for the aging? Patisserie became a luxury item as well. Mother finally found a way of using some of the flour allotment other than baking a "Wähe" on Friday. She baked a "Gugelhopf" for some of our birthdays. This success spurred her on to repeat it on some Sundays based on the false assumption that my (fussy eater) brother was especially fond of it. I wonder where she got the butter and eggs. Somehow, she always knew where and how to find the ingredients she wanted or needed. This included the daily piece of meat, but she didn't have to resort to horse meat which was sold at half coupon three houses down from us (and whose butcher got filthy rich). We kids hardly ever ate meat and I don't remember if Dad ever had to observe the two officially decreed meatless days—Wednesdays and Fridays.

But then he was absent now for long stretches of time. As soon as we had those Swiss papers, he was conscripted into the "Hilfsarmee" (support army) as a clerk in a beautiful but supposedly secret location, which later turned out to be general headquarters. He must have enjoyed this phase of his life—he came on leave an animated man and, suddenly, a wine connoisseur. To me his wearing nailed boots, apparently the only required piece of uniform aside from an armband, seemed strange. But after all, he had been a mountain climber before we were born and was quite at ease with those clunkers.

His business, like many other retail stores, came to a virtual standstill. I have been told that no photographic material was available, and I bet taking pictures entailed a certain security risk. Mother was left in charge despite her limited technical knowledge. In order to make ends meet, she appropriated a room in our spacious apartment and started to sell "Persian" rugs (machine-made ones) and "Occasionen" (second-hand items) including our toys and clothes ( which, according to her assessment, were no longer needed) from more prosperous days. The car, an Adler convertible, went too; and did we ever cry real tears. I still see it rolling down the Grüngasse. Later, from economic necessity, even we had to move from there. Dad bought and settled us in one of the many houses some Jews had to sell in order to finance their emigration to the States. At the time, Mr. Goldman was very grateful for the speedy transaction. And we eventually became reconciled to the much smaller and by comparison somewhat primitive accommodations.

These events somehow seemed more traumatic than the periodic howl of the sirens, which sprung up all over on strategic house tops to warn of bomb attacks. There were quite a few of these raids once the Brits and Americans started to use Swiss airspace to fly to Italy. The incidents were too strategic to be called mistakes, and even though the U.S. paid for the damages, it couldn't resurrect the victims.

From our blacked out living room my father and I watched tracer bombs falling out of the sky one night. Usually we merely heard the droning of squadrons of heavy planes after an alert. But this sight and the subsequent explosions compelled us to run to our air raid shelter. This was an obligatory installation in every house, with heavy beams supporting the ceiling, concrete walls and a vault-like door.

At night Switzerland became black except for the headlights of emergency vehicles on the streets. Our lives were conducted behind shutters and curtains reinforced with black lining. If the smallest rays of light escaped, we could expect the block warden to ring the doorbell and issue a warning. Not understanding about pacifism, I was scandalized that my former confirmation preacher refused to obey the blackout orders. He spent many days in jail for his principles and unrepentant behavior. I suppose people considered him to be one of those hateful Nazi sympathizers (even though it was at Germany's behest that we blacked out). Many a family was split because of them—a chapter almost too painful to remember. That uncle, not much older than I, brainwashed with a whole bunch of other students at the university, deserted the army, wrote form letters praising the Führer, swam across the Rhine and was eventually killed at the Ostfront. This left my forever-grieving grandmother searching for a possible grandchild somewhere in Germany. She contacted (and asked me to accompany her) any "Hellseher" (medium) she could locate to obtain information or leads. They all kept her hopes alive.

We mostly listened to radio Beromünster, not trusting the propaganda of foreign senders and felt fairly optimistic until the Maginot Line collapsed. After that nothing, neither the concrete "teeth," read blocks, sprouting in the fields to stop a tank invasion, nor the camouflaged bunkers and airplane hangars seemed a deterrent against the Wehrmacht. Besides, the army had decided to guard the frontiers and primarily defend the alpine reduit while in a sense sacrificing the Mittelland, where defense was largely left in local volunteer hands. Despite Hitler's promises to respect our neutrality, we knew, that if he wanted, he could easily overrun us with our small arsenal of anti-aircraft guns and few planes. Perhaps the fact that bigwigs had to secure a place to find refuge, to stow their money, to conduct secret meetings, and to use Swiss diplomatic services kept us out of harm's way. And indeed Alan Dulles' secret service was active in Switzerland beginning in 1942.

After the armistice with France a councilor, Pilet-Golaz, hinted in so many words, that we might be better off throwing in our lot with Germany in anticipation of a changed Europe. General Guisan, head of the army, assembled the higher echelon on the famous Rütli and they all swore to defend the country against any dangers. This allayed fears that had pervaded not only the populace but the military as well—that the government might adjust its direction to Germany instead of retaining its neutrality.

Most of the issues, which nowadays are bandied about vis-à-vis Switzerland, were not publicly discussed or known, as far as I remember. Perhaps I was too young to be interested in trade embargoes or money laundering. But then, I just recently became aware that as of September 1939 the army had oversight of the press and that while the Red Cross knew about the concentration camps, it kept quiet. Yet despite all the accusations hurled against Switzerland these days, I marvel at how Bern juggled the conflicting interests of all parties in order to stay out of the conflagration. After all, we were totally surrounded. In hindsight it is easy to throw stones.

We did know of refugees—300,000 of them, practically the size of Zurich then. Among them were

- 1,700 interned U.S. airmen and 158 of their bombers
- 13,000 interned Poles who fought in France and helped construct the Sustenpass
- Hungarian Jews who were threatened with genocide, an issue apparently hotly, but secretly, discussed on governmental levels.

We knew we had to knit those socks for our soldiers, and be thankful for our ever becoming more expensive food, while others began to scavenge and starve. We ordinary people did not know of the caviar and other exotic delicacies a disgruntled lady accused me of having wallowed in. In truth we often wondered how long our provisions would last. Despite the fact that arable land had been doubled, meat rations were cut to 2 kilos a month. The "old aunts," a Swiss Navy of secondhand freighters, brought in grain, oil and coffee from non-aligned countries.

We knew because we heard heavily camouflaged trains rumbling through the night—many with Italian writing and German songs emanating from others. We saw and met French children taking holidays (like Fresh Air children) with families or alone in camps. One summer my brother's boy scout troop cooked in one of these, then modern, and as far as he was concerned, luxurious camps. Coincidently, at this very camp recent refugees from the Balkans went on strike because they considered the updated accommodations to be inhuman. One French teenager joined our class. Struggling with German, she asked one day for "castrated" coffee at the grocer's. We thought she had solved her problem brilliantly, not knowing the word for caffeine free. Then a teenage cousin from Germany also managed to R and R with my grandparents. She had to return unhappily, not having achieved her design of snagging a Swiss husband. But she did all right for herself: She married a famous German opera singer.

Many of our male teachers were also called up and were replaced with retirees, especially women. Teenage pupils spent summer vacations on farms, working for the women left in charge while the men were in the army. Manpower was short with all the extra acreage under cultivation. Victory gardens (now sought after spots—an escape from the noise of the city to an oasis of flowers and lettuce) were found on factory grounds and even schoolyards. Our 11th and 12th grade weeklong school excursions to soak up culture in foreign countries were replaced by tours to historical Swiss sites. We never got a glimpse of the Matterhorn since it remained veiled during our two-day stay in Zermatt.

Intercontinental mail service was severely disrupted. Often whole packets of letters from the same country, but postmarked on different days or months, arrived in the same mail, sometimes mixed with letters from totally different parts of the world. A canary yellow, heavy wool jacket, knit by an aunt in Australia, took over a year to reach me. The color was too outrageous for a conservative Swiss teenager. I never wore it, besides it was too large. The wool, however, was certainly of a quality we had never seen before. It would have kept me warm.

The often boring Sunday drives were replaced by even more boring family walks to the lake and some café to have gelato (water ice). The Sunday dress all of a sudden became an important item since it was so publicly paraded. I would sit for hours drawing designs and then fret over which one to have our "Schniideri" (dressmaker) execute. There was this one particular red number . . . This dressmaker, who for some reason could swear in Arabic, always made me one dress for each season; but why we employed her, I really do not know. Perhaps ready-to-wear apparel is an after the war development

VE Day, the day Germany surrendered, is one of my most vivid memories. School was dismissed after a rare celebratory assembly at 10 a.m. I walked on air to the market on my way home and spontaneously blew my saved up meager allowances on the largest bouquet of flowers I could afford.

There were sequels to this war—being cited to welcome survivors of concentration camps, which were now public knowledge. Gratefully we were only required to wave at their arriving trains. I think I would have fainted if I had gotten any closer to what appeared to be skeletons with big hollow eyes. But then the visiting U.S. Army bands also moved me to tears. How could these unmartial, sprightly-looking and marching men, playing Glen Miller, a novelty to my ears, have fought such a terrible war on beaches and in trenches? I had an idea of the war now that I turned eighteen, the legal milestone for admittance to "real" movies with newsreels. Before then it had been strictly Shirley Temple if accompanied by an adult to a matinee. Interestingly there seemed to be no age limit for operas or theater; and we enjoyed some of the best actors and the works of the most creative dramatists during this period. A USO was established by the American colony and we came face to face with black people. There were CARE packages with SPAM (is it edible?). Old letters trickled in, and life went on.

# Winter

A mere 70 years ago, it was still up to most families to keep their own living space warm during the cold months. Central heating was rare, oil and gas heat unknown. Firewood, coal and "briquettes" (coke) were the fuels of the day.

The wood was delivered in bundles of "Schiitli" (split logs), the coal in burlap bags by black dusted men in leather tabbards with hoods. They toted their loads from the truck down the cellar stairs on their shoulder or backs. Each family in the apartment house had a space, fenced in floor to ceiling, with a padlocked door in the basement. From this cache of fuel someone, generally mother, hauled the daily supply to feed the tiled stoves in their individual apartments. Most of these "Kachelofen" (stoves) heated two rooms simultaneously, being part of a wall and protruding into two bedrooms at the same time, or the kitchen and the living room. The bathroom without the tub (you took your bath in the washkitchen or a public bath once a week) remained cold, as did the bedrooms very often, especially during the war. But to compensate we had those billowy featherbeds (which Frau Holle of fairytale shook to make snow) . . . and even running water in the sinks. When my mother was young, she often had to break through a layer of ice to get to the water in the porcelain basin, on the washstand of every bedroom in her days, to do her morning toilette. But like her, we dressed and undressed under the covers. Unlike her, though, we did not have to go on Sunday kindling- and pinecone-gathering expeditions with our father to cut down on fuel costs. Nor did we go berry- and mushroom-picking to reduce household expenses.

Our own apartment, together with two stores on the first floor were centrally heated with coal. So our much larger supply for the immense burners were chuted through an open basement window to a storage bin, floating coal dust for days on cellar floor and steps, and to be tracked all over the rest of the house.

Of course, the coal and wood soot emanating from so many chimneys tinged new fallen snow a dirty gray within days. Therefore, the ever cleaning conscious hausfrau hurried to lay out as many of her oriental rugs as possible, face down, onto the pristine white and gave them a good beating with the "Teppich-chlopfer" (rug beater), now hard to find. The carpets emerged from this ritual restored with brighter colors. They left behind their dirt in dark rectangles all over courtyards.

Streets were, if at all, not plowed down to the surface. Tire chains were necessary since snow tires still had to be developed. Some

delivery people, especially farmers, hauled out their sleds. Men and boys wore shoes with hobnails which in summer facilitated climbing mountains; women and girls resorted to high rubber boots. Many windowsills sported bird feeders or were sprinkled with bread crumbs. Even horses and dogs were protected against the cold by heavy blanket covers.

Every once in a while you might hear a loud crashing noise, especially on a sunny day: Part of the snow cover had slid from a roof, or icicles broke from eaves down onto the sidewalk. People began walking close to the edge of a sidewalk hoping to avoid being hit.

# Santa Claus
## (Samichlaus, December 6, Evening)

Santa in Switzerland was not a fixture in department stores where children could sit on his lap and recite their wishes into his ear. He was far from a benign, jolly, rotund character.

Our Santa appeared on December 6, not on a reindeer-drawn sled, but on foot or on a bicycle (the war was on and gasoline for cars was reserved for more important missions). He came to visit children whose parents had hired him as a kind of scout for the "Chrischtchindli" who would visit later, on December 24, to herald the start of the Christmas celebration.

It took a multitude of Santas to visit so many children. Some Santas had advertised themselves in want-ads as "child-loving," others as "authoritarian" and "awe-inspiring." Somehow, though, they all followed the same script. Instead of coming down the chimney (we had no fireplaces) they stomped up the mostly wood on stairs of the apartment building in heavy shoes and knocked threateningly on the hall door. There our parents, mom mostly, received them, handed them goodies and divulged secrets about our deportment, while we kids quaked behind the closed living room door, rehearsing little verses which we were expected to recite before Santa opened his sack to distribute "his" bounty.

In his usually red suit, Santa always made a theatrical entrance into the living room. He hardly ever sat down. So, towering over us he questioned us with his basso voice about our behavior in the past year. If we happened to forget a "sin," he was quick to remind us, having been prompted by a parent. We were instructed to be truthful since he would report to the Christmas Angel who would then adjust our wishlist commensurate with how we stacked up in his estimation. We had placed this wishlist between the slats of the closed window shutters some night prior to Santa's visit, so that the angel could fly by and collect it. Of course, the list had always vanished when we checked the next morning.

After our confessions and recital of the poem, and after he had lectured us according to instructions, it was time to receive his benificence, nuts, mandarins, a candy bar and certainly a gingerbread Santa cookie with his colorful picture pasted on top. The shares went according to how good we had been. Woe to the out of control child: He or she was threatened to be stuck, head first, into the very sack

from which Santa had produced his gifts; they would then be taken downstairs where Schmutzly , the wild and dark helper was waiting with Santa's donkey (supposedly). Schmutzly would throw the bag over the donkey and together with Santa take the child to Santa's cabin deep in the woods, to stay until it learned to behave appropriately. While this threat was never carried out, it was a terrifying behavior modifier and certainly made one shake with fright the following year in anticipation of Santa's visit.

As a last gesture, before his departure, Santa might have handed the parents a Fitze, a switch, which became a fixture behind a mirror as an intimidating reminder to behave or have a sore behind. I was especially frightened by Santa even though theoretically I had nothing to fear. I often forgot my lines or jumbled them—even though I knew my haul would be larger than my brother's, which of course made me very popular with him. But why should it not? While I fretted before and after Santa's visit, he and his gang of friends were out deflating as many Santa bicycle tires as they could locate. Yet, miraculously he was always at home at the right time for Santa and flawlessly recited a verse like:

| Santa Niggi Näggi | Santa Nicki Nack |
| Hinderem Ofe schtecki | behind the oven I am hiding |
| Gimmer Nuss und Birre | Gimme nuts and a pear |
| Dänn chummi wieder füre | then I'll reappear |

My brother probably secretly enjoyed the suffering of his 4-year-old sister who still believed in the Easter bunny. But if we had offered Santa a glass of milk and a plate of cookies, he might have been a friendlier visitor, rather than one we were relieved to see disappear.

And I am still puzzled as to the real identity of the Christchindli. Especially now that my daughter quizzes me. Is the Christ child Baby Jesus as the name implies—but then why has he been turned into an angel flying around, collecting wishlists? And has become in most imaginations a female, to boot? Of course this Chrischtchindli disappears from the horizon just like the Easter rabbit at a certain stage of a child's life. Therefore, no further explanation may be required. Subsequently the birth of Christ is celebrated in age-old pagan fashion of exchanging gifts to celebrate winter solstice—while singing Christian carols.

# Winter Fun in the City in the 30's

My winter memories of the city are gray, gray . . . more gray and a faint smell of soot, low hanging clouds and a desire of never having to go outside. Unless, of course, it had just snowed and the sun came out and everything seemed bright for a few days. Until the white turned gray as well.

If it had not been for those occasional interludes of snow, life would indeed have been even more boring without television, computer or books for that matter. No wonder most of us were sent to bed around eight or before, but after homework. Those rare bright days, though, energized us to rummage for our sleds in the basement or under the roof where there was more storage space for apartment dwellers. We all knew of some hill or steep street where we could pull them up to schuss down, over and over again. There were few opportunities for skiing in the city proper. Few of us owned skis anyway, contrary to the notion that all Swiss ski (or yodel; even fewer of us can do that successfully). However, if we were among the lucky ones in a skiing family, we had to wait for a Sunday to be taken to some higher-lying ground outside the city. The exodus of skiers often necessitated running special trains to accommodate them all. We assiduously practiced our "christies" and "Stemmbööge" on the "idiot hills" until we were allowed to graduate to the longer pistes. A lot of trudging was involved. Skilifts were just coming into fashion in the more prestigious resorts, frequented by the English mostly. They set the trend for the modern ski culture with the après ski happy hour, fashions, smoking . . . Most of us day trippers were satisfied with an action-filled day and a suntan as a bonus. Wow, the girls got to wear pants!—heavy, almost felt-like black numbers which kept us dry in spills. None of this streamlined, colorful synthetic stuff  nor fancy boots and bindings. Our "Brätter" (slats) were attached to ordinary hightop shoes with springs and strips of leather.

The Swiss hockey team fired our imagination in those days. We followed their matches passionately via radio broadcasts, and got very indignant over the tactics of the Canadian and Czech teams who played rough.

Many boys loved to emulate their idols, but there were few realistic opportunities to practice the sport, unless a school flooded its playing field so it might freeze into a makeshift rink. Some boys sported those black hockey skates, but most had to be content with screw-on shoe types which were adjustable to fit a few years' worth of growing shoe sizes. A greater number of girls skated than skied. Sonja Henje was their role model. Most of them,though, also had to do with those screw-on skates rather than Kunst-Schleifschuhe (skating art skates). These white leather hightops with attached skates (as we know them now) had distinct snob appeal, especially when worn with white stockings and a swirly skirt. "Professional" skates were bought a few sizes too large, for us to grow into. Time to get new ones was when our toes finally froze because there was no stuffing (perhaps a sock) left to insulate them against the cold.

The one artificial rink in town was rather far from public transportation. Yet hordes of kids made a pilgrimage there on the free Wednesday and Saturday afternoons. Others were left to their own devices: They drowned a section of the courtyard with water hoping that cold temperatures would cooperate and freeze it into an icy surface on which to slide.

Snowball fights were the easiest and fastest way to organize some action. Theories as to how to obtain the most efficient weapon ran from burying a stone in the middle, to dunking it in water for an icy surface . . . and above all, having an adequate supply of balls handy before the battle. Which preferably was fought from behind snowbrick walls, cowboy style. (One of my uncles scared me when I was little: His nose had been flattened by one of those missiles and he carried the consequences all his life.)

Girls were more into building snowmen. Coal for the eyes was still easy to come by and carrots (for the nose) a traditional winter vegetable. Ambitious boys constructed igloos which often became ad hoc clubhouses, furnished with mats and sometimes kerosene lanterns. Girls might gain admission to this fraternity with offers of food.

Of course not all families were sports-minded. But even they would experience the need to get from under this oppressive gray into some sunshine. Sunday hikes up a nearby mountain, high enough to break through the cloud ceiling, to breathe more freely, became a ritual for some. After an early morning climb, while the adults identified other peaks escaping the "Nebelmeer" (sea of fog), the kids impatiently waited for the moment when they were treated to hot chocolate and a Nussgipfel (filled Danish), or a sausage with potato salad, depending on whether they patronized a swanky hotel or a popular taproom with smoke-filled rooms at the summit.

Cognizant of the scarcity of winter sport activities for most city children, local school boards organized Skilager (camps) at nominal cost where kids were outfitted with the necessary equipment. Yet even this measure excluded some. But they did have a week's vacation while the others enjoyed "Skiferien". Perhaps they went to the lake and fed the hungry gulls and swans with stale pieces of bread and wished that the lake would freeze . . . now, not only once or twice in their lifetime.

# Schuelsylveschter
## (Last Day of School Prior to the Christmas Break)

It might have been foggy, cold or drizzling, but it was after five in the morning and certainly still dark outside. On this day, however, most children were wide awake after a night of fitful sleep, eager to get dressed and leave the apartment in order to take part in the yearly ritual of waking up the neighborhood with an unholy racket just before the Christmas vacation, which usually coincided with winter solstice.

The kids emerged, for once bundled up without having been reminded, dented pot lids in hand, to be used as cymbals. Whistles, toy trumpets, drums, cowbells, cap pistols and a few harmless firecrackers joined the cacophony of noise. Alone or in gangs, the kids haunted the streets, ringing apartment bells as they roamed leisurely, but fleeing quickly before an irate adult could douse them with a bucket full of cold water. They excited dogs to bark, chased cats up trees. The newspaper woman delivering the first of three daily editions into mailboxes, knew that shaking her head, wagging her finger or verbal admonishments would not calm things down . . . but watched her cart, often an old baby carriage, with hawkeyes.

In fact, this morning nobody really expected the youngsters to obey—they reigned supreme. They might have run from a potentially punitive situation, only to regroup at another corner to continue their noise-making mission. And that is what it essentially was, even without their being aware of it: As in pagan times, they were attempting to drive out the darkness which had been gobbling up more and more of the daylight. Noise works every time.

The bedlam was continued until it was time to go to class at eight o'clock. Few went home for breakfast because nobody wanted to risk being the Sylvester and the butt of jokes, that is, being the last one to get into the classroom.

Guess who most likely turned out to be this Sylvester? A girl, of course. Few of us were allowed to join in the fun and challenge by fathers who remembered their youthful antics.

Sylvester was a nuisance for late sleepers. But it was innocent fun compared to what happens nowadays. Letterboxes are set on fire, cars vandalized, explosives set off in containers. No more simple potlids, paper lanterns or whistles. To stem the tide of this modern mayhem,

schools arrange all-night parties under supervision or offer free swimming in the city's indoor pool. All in an effort to keep the celebrants from being harmed or causing trouble.

Sylvester is what the Swiss call December 31, the last day of the year. So it makes sense to have applied the same name to the last school day in the same year.

# Wienacht
# Christmas Celebration Starting December 24

The Christmas Eve dinner always seemed later and longer than the customary one, more special too—a chicken with pommes frites instead of buttered bread, cold cuts and cheese. Yet we kids were actually too nervous to appreciate the menu change. We wanted the meal over and done with, and who cared if the dishes were done and put away? Mother did, of course. For once she had eager volunteers. Anticipation mounted with each perfunctorily dried plate or fork until she finally took off her apron and disappeared into the living room. It had been locked mysteriously for days and the keyhole was covered from the inside against spying eyes. We kids, too, had locked our own rooms from time to time in order to work in secret on presents for our parents. We embroidered, crocheted or even sawed, and often felt like bursting with the desire to divulge the nature of the project we were working on. Naturally we tried to elicit clues about the status of the presents we were expecting. After all, we had submitted our wishlist and posted it outside a window for the Christkind to collect. We had such contradictory ideas of where the presents actually came from. The fact that we were hardly aware whether our parents were preparing for Christmas heightened our anxieties with each day. Except for our baking cookies, especially Mailänderli (a sugar cookie which we were sometimes allowed to decorate conservatively) and the Christmas tree markets, there were few other signs of the approaching event. Show windows might have been decorated festively a few days before Christmas; no public displays of nativity scenes, no music carols in the stores or elevators; no strings of colored lights; they were reserved for summer beer gardens.

Nevertheless, Christmas excitement was in the air, especially after the appearance of Santa Claus. And never more so than now, with mother and dad in the living room while we were waiting in front of the still-locked door for the tingling of the silver bell . . . announcing that the Christkind had finished her preparations . . . and the door was about to open for us to ohh and ahh beholding the tree, lit with a dozen candles or more, weighted down with glass ornaments, tinsel and angel hair and . . . nuts, chocolate pine cones and perhaps a sparkler or two. Naturally the pile of presents was the true object of our enthusiasm.

So much waiting seemed to surround Christmas, so much being on pins and needles. Even the weeks between successively lighting the four candles, one for each Sunday before Christmas, on the Advent wreath, seemed interminably drawn out. And now, when we were almost at the point of getting our hands on the presents, we first had to sing, or rather accompany the grammophone records playing "Stille Nacht" or "O Tannenbaum." Unfortunately the canned singers always knew all the verses to each carol. We might even have to talk to the Christmas angel herself, as long as we believed in the myth. (I remember the day she became demystified for me. She had been so lovely, all in white, standing next to the tree with huge wings, talking to me so sweetly. And then she almost floated away. I ran across the terrace to our neighbors dying to tell them of the miracle. Only to find this angel with a glass of wine in hand, telling her audience how awestruck I had been and therefore had failed to recognize her.)

So the Christmas magic was sometimes mixed with disappointment. Who needed an aquarium full of fish when you had wished for a real live monkey? Or a piano, when you had your heart set on a record player or your own radio?

The parents, though, never seemed to complain, silently or out loud. Their gifts were predictably the same, year after year. A new apron for mother, hand-knit socks for father. An occasional nightgown or a pair of pajamas, a sweater or a tie and whatever we children had dreamed up, a handkerchief with fancy edging, clothes hangers covered with knitted sleeves, a leather case for keys or a wooden board to hang them on. No matter what, our offerings, clumsily wrapped, were received with expressions of surprise and appreciation. Mom and dad celebrated with a slice of grandma's stollen and a late cup of coffee while we were allowed to stay up long past our usual 7:30 bedtime until we heard the bells of the Catholic church summoning the faithful to midnight mass.

Christmas is a two-day holiday. So we could sleep in and still had some surprises to look forward to. The second day meant visits to grandparents and relatives. We did not mind singing around their Christmas trees, candle lit but carefully watched when the early evening fell. We had our main loot.

The week after Christmas the mail delivered bright New Year's greetings. Small cards somewhat longer than our credit cards, with pictures of snow-covered landscapes, drawings of pigs, chimney sweeps, and four leaf clovers (all symbols of good luck), on one half and carrying the customary wishes for a good New Year on the other. I wonder what happened to my collection of these little treasures.

# Grandma's Stollen

Aside from the Christmas tree and "Stille Nacht" ("Silent Night") America has adopted among others the Christmas stollen as a holiday custom with German roots. While it is widely sold, I have met only a few people who claim to like it. Until I came to this country, I had seldom tasted any variation of the original Dresden recipe. During her lifetime my Saxon grandmother was our sole source of this traditional "bread." I understand why people don't a priori take to it. (A similar fate befalls fruitcake and plum pudding.) We kids were actually exposed to the real thing (I suppose) via a detour—Grandma always baked Streuselkuchen for us to feast on, a strategy to make the pièce de résistance go further for the adults. One by one we had the courage to ask for admittance to that chosen circle and developed a discriminating taste for her ever so solemnly rationed-out buttery delicacy. "Rationed," because in theory a stollen should last until Easter. But it never does, neither Grandma's nor now, a local Bulgarian lady's (taught by her East German husband), who, thank goodness, can hold her own next to Grandma's any day. And "solemn," by the way, is not too exaggerated an expression in conjunction with Grandma stollen.

Stollen was elevated to a ritual in her home starting early in December. Ordering hunks of butter and changing the water of the tub in which they were kept fresh; cutting citron into small pieces; chopping almonds, some bitter; clearing surfaces for resting the plethora of rising loaves, and readying linen to cover them with: This usually serene woman turned into a whirling dervish. She never tolerated anyone in her vicinity during the production phase. She declared the kitchen and "Gute Stube" (parlor) off limits for days and even closed her store at times. And woe to whoever slammed a door, thus jeopardizing the success of her creation by causing the seasoning dough to fall. We practically tiptoed around, should we have visited during this crucial period.

Grandma's reclusiveness in a way has cheated me out of continuing and handing down the family tradition. I have no idea of the stollen secrets except that butter from non-homogenized milk is required for the genuine article. (This bit was actually divulged by an "insider," a baker whom we patronized after Grandma's death.) Also flour stored in a wardrobe with camphor balls, as she had done one year to safeguard her monthly allotment during the war, is a definite no-no. But since her stollen was so sacrosanct, nobody ever commented on the peculiar taste of that year's batch. Nobody as much as batted an eyelash when she served the customary thick slices at coffee time. (Unfortunately the grandkids' chocolate bars had also acquired the same camphor aroma . . . so that her sons for once were the only ones truly appreciative of their present: A camphory pair of hand-knit black socks. No moths!) Despite our conspiratorial silence, Grandma knew.

We never had camphory stollen again.

If other grandmothers left the younger generations also to guess about which ingredient and how much of it to knead into this tradition, no wonder there are so many variations of the Dresden stollen theme on the Christmas market. Or did the progeny change the recipe for economic and dietary reasons? The original is certainly sinfully rich.

Thus, stollen not being in my purview, I adopted for our family in the U.S. a bona fide gingerbread house as a holiday tradition. The fun is in the designing and decorating of the concoction, not in the assembly. The melted sugar "glue" invariably raises painful blisters. Nor was there enjoyment in the eating—the structure becomes too hard, but at least the candy can be pried loose. The finished product looks good as a centerpiece. But so do the shortcut, graham cracker covered, milk and juice carton editions, or the ones made from catalogue kits. And they do not exactly require burns as stamps of approval, declaring them "homemade." We'll see how this tradition, if at all, will be carried on—gingerbread space stations?

With this last paragraph I have crossed into yet another era and space – adulthood in the U.S. In logical progression therefore, this chronicling of childhood memories has to now be handed over to the next generation. It was fun recalling a past, some of which seemed to have slipped from memory but was resurrected for good or ill by "Esel's Brugge" (literally donkey bridges) or associations.